YOU AND YOUR TEENAGER

A parent's guide to making the most
of the teen years

Dr John Court

with illustrations by Paul Stanish

Angus&Robertson
An imprint of HarperCollins*Publishers*

All the case notes quoted in this book are based on the author's experience,
but details are so changed that anyone who may think they can identify themself
or someone they know will almost certainly be wrong.

Angus & Robertson
An imprint of HarperCollins*Publishers*, Australia

First published in Australia in 1995

HarperCollins*Publishers*
25 Ryde Road, Pymble, Sydney NSW 2073, Australia
31 View Road, Auckland 10, New Zealand
77–85 Fulham Palace Road, London W6 8JB, United Kingdom
Hazelton Lanes, 55 Avenue Road, Suite 2900, Toronto, Ontario M5R 3L2
and 1995 Markham Road, Scarborough, Ontario M1B 5M8, Canada
10 East 53rd Street, New York NY 10032, USA

National Library of Australia Cataloguing-in-Publication data:

Court, John M. (John Maurice), 1929- .
   You and your teenager.

   Bibliography.
   Includes index.
   ISBN 0 207 18756 8.

   1. Teenagers. 2. Parent and teenager. I. Title.

649.125

Illustrations by Paul Stanish

Printed in Hong Kong

9 8 7 6 5 4 3 2 1
99 98 97 96 95

Contents

About the author

Dr John Court is a paediatric physician specializing in adolescent health.

He has spent most of his professional life in Australia, apart from periods in the United Kingdom on study leave in London and Birmingham, and has been a regular lecturer in Malaysia, Singapore, Hong Kong, China and Japan.

His principal interests have been in the area of growth and development in childhood and adolescence, with particular concern for young people with chronic illnesses as they pass from childhood to adult life.

He was Editor for many years of the *Australian Paediatric Journal*, and is currently Editor in Chief of the international *Journal of Paediatrics and Child Health*. Since 1993 he has been Editor of the *Newsletter of the International Association for Adolescent Health*. Dr Court has been published widely in scientific and medical journals and books.

He was a Foundation Member and later President of the Australian Association for Adolescent Health. He developed a medical service for adolescents at Melbourne's Royal Children's Hospital, and this has since been incorporated into The Centre for Adolescent Health in Melbourne, where he is Senior Physician.

In 1993 his work with adolescents, particularly those with diabetes, was recognized with the award of Member of the Order of Australia.

Acknowledgements

The author has known very many teenagers. Through sharing their personal experiences, they have all contributed to his understanding of adolescence.

This book is dedicated to them all and especially to Andrew, Jane and Madeleine.

Introduction

Teenagers are great. Teenagers are fun. Teenagers are funny. They keep you young.

Well, not all of them. And not all the time. Sometimes they drive you mad. Often they hasten your decline into nagging middle age with their refusal to listen to reason. They are personally responsible for grey hairs appearing before they should. You want to help them with their problems and worries but they won't let you. And they are so strong and active, why can't they help around the house more? At least they could keep their rooms clean and tidy. Why won't they get up in the morning, and what on earth do they spend their money on?

One day you could cheerfully wring their necks. The next day they give you a hug and tell you about their worries and you could weep for your love of them and your inability to solve their teenage problems. They are so big, but deep down they are just kids.

What's happening to them? Is it all hormones and growing up? Are they normal? Will they grow out of it? Or is something really the matter with your teenage child and their awful moods? Is it your fault? What did you do wrong? Perhaps they have fallen into the wrong company. Would you really know if they were using drugs? They learn so much about sex these days at school and from the media — how can you help them to keep some balance in their lives and protect them from getting hurt?

Maybe it can help you to understand your children going through puberty and adolescence, and to help them yourself, if you know what is normal and usual in this unique period of life. That way you may be able to get along with them more comfortably, and work out if there really is something wrong. And when they need help (which they will sometimes), you can give that help in a way they can respond to, and perhaps find additional help if they need that too.

Remember: Most teenagers are perfectly healthy and their behaviour is normal. Some conflict is usual in the home but most teenage conflict with parents and siblings is about relatively minor things. After all, parents seldom agree on everything themselves, and it's about how the conflict is resolved that really matters. Teenagers are usually pretty resilient, and provided that you as a parent can hang in with them, and give support when they need it, they will emerge as responsible and sane adults.

This book is about helping you (and them) get there.

CHAPTER 1

PUBERTY

The start of adolescence

ADOLESCENCE SEEMS TO BE STARTING EARLIER AND GOING ON LONGER

The start of puberty seems to be getting earlier and earlier in children today. A century ago a girl might expect her first period at the age of 16. Today the average age for a girl's periods to start is just before her thirteenth birthday. Many children in primary school have started puberty at the age of 10 or 11 when they are in all other ways still young children. Many are not really ready for the emotional upheavals of adolescence at this age, particularly as there is often a wide difference in development between one child and another in these early years.

To make matters worse, adolescence seems to be extending to a later and later age. When does it stop? Some parents despair that their young adult offspring will ever grow up, particularly if they don't leave home or are still continuing studies in their early twenties.

Puberty is said to start with the first signs of sexual development. This might be when breast buds first develop in a girl or the testes start to enlarge in a boy. Usually we find that pubic hair starts to grow at about the same time (sometimes just before and sometimes a bit after the other signs).

The slow process of adolescent development proceeds over the next 5 to 10 years and comes to an end when the young person is socially and emotionally mature. This is usually some time after sexual development is complete, often years later, and depends to a large extent on social and cultural circumstances. Many years of study or training and late entry to the workforce have usually led to a longer period of reliance on family support and tolerance within the family home. And this has meant a longer period of adolescent transition to adult life.

WHEN SHOULD PUBERTY BEGIN?

There is no correct time for puberty to start: it is different for each child, and being early or a bit late to start puberty often runs in families. The girl who hasn't started menstruating till she is over 14 may find that her mother was also late. The boy who hasn't much to show for pubertal development at 15 may find that his father was late too (but his father may have forgotten when he started puberty, because there isn't an obvious event like menstruation for him to remember).

Average ages for the start of puberty aren't very helpful — after all, who is 'average'?

Perhaps it is more helpful to say that *most* girls will have started breast development by age 13 years. This means that 95% of girls will have done so, but it also means that 5% will not, and most of these late starters will be perfectly normal. In the same way *most* girls will have had their first period by age 15, but there will still be many perfectly normal, healthy girls who have not. It also means that if a girl's periods have not started by age 15, or breast development has not appeared by (say) 13, and if she is worried, it is perfectly reasonable to seek advice from your doctor, both to check it out and also to reassure her.

A very early start of puberty can be even more worrying for a girl or her parents. Some breast development in infancy is common and is usually of no consequence, disappearing by about age 6 or earlier. Apart from this, however, if there is breast development before age 9 it would be wise to consult your doctor, even though it may still be quite normal. The development of pubic hair before age 9 is not usually normal and should be investigated medically in case there is an hormonal imbalance.

For boys, late development of puberty is much more common, but can still cause a lot of embarrassment and distress. Most boys (95% of them) will have signs of puberty, with pubic hair and enlargement of the testes, by age 14. If there is no sign of development at this age, and if the boy is worried or unhappy about this, it is perfectly reasonable to seek advice from your doctor.

As in girls, very early development of puberty in a boy may be a sign of hormone imbalance, and should be investigated. If pubic hair develops, or if there is growth of the penis before age 10, it would be sensible to seek advice from your doctor.

THE TIMING OF EVENTS DURING PUBERTY

The sexual and physical changes of puberty tend to follow a common sequence: you can usually predict what is happening, and what will happen next. What you can't do is predict how *fast* changes will occur and whether it will take just two or three years to complete physical development, or whether it will take many more years. Many factors affect the rate of physical development at this time. The main factor is usually genetic (i.e. inherited from the parents), and affects such things as the timing of when puberty starts. Other factors that may influence the rate of development are nutrition (inadequate nutrition slows it down), chronic illness (such as severe asthma, which may also slow it down, especially if it is hard to control), intense physical activity (training for competition gymnastics, for instance, may slow puberty down) and emotional distress, particularly if it leads to poor eating habits.

The timing of puberty is different for girls and boys. Girls tend to start puberty about 18 months earlier than boys, and may reach sexual and social maturity a little earlier too. This varies a lot from one child to another. The timing of growth also differs between girls and boys: for instance, girls tend to have their growth spurt earlier than boys, so there is a short period when girls tend to be a little taller than boys of their own age. Boys soon catch up, however, and keep on growing for a longer time.

So the timing of puberty — when it starts, how long it takes, and whether it is proceeding normally — can be a worry for some children and teenagers. When should you seek advice? The obvious answer is when you or your son or daughter is worried. If things are just a variation of normal, it is easy to reassure you. If there is doubt, it is usually easy to work out what is happening. Your doctor may perhaps suggest referral to an endocrinologist (a hormone specialist), particularly one who specializes in children and adolescents.

When would it be reasonable to have things checked out, even if you aren't particularly worried? The following might be a guide:

- A girl hasn't shown signs of breast development by the age of 13½.

- A girl hasn't had a period by the age of 15.
- A boy hasn't developed any signs of puberty by age 14.
- A girl has shown signs of breast development before age 9 years.
- A boy has shown signs of puberty before age 10 years.

Puberty in a boy

PHYSICAL DEVELOPMENT

There are many physical changes taking place in a boy during puberty and adolescence. Some are very obvious to everyone, like the spurt in growth and the long limbs and large feet. Some are mainly obvious (and of great interest) to the boy himself, such as the development of pubic hair and growth of his penis. Some changes, such as increased levels of hormones circulating in the blood and the rise in blood pressure, are not obvious at all but may be important to a doctor concerned about the boy's health.

These changes are occurring over a period of years and tend to follow a similar sequence in all boys. It is important, of course, for a doctor — especially one who specializes in hormones and puberty development and growth (a paediatric endocrinologist) — to know about this sequence. It may also be helpful for parents, and for teenagers themselves, to understand these changes. This helps to reassure them that all is going well (even if it seems a bit slow for some boys) or to pick up anything that may not be going well so they can get medical advice before major problems develop.

THE BRAIN SENDS SIGNALS WHEN IT'S TIME TO START PUBERTY

Long before any changes have become obvious, the body is getting ready for puberty by producing hormones to stimulate the testes to develop. These hormones are made in the brain and act as messengers to tell other glands that the time has come for sexual maturation to start. We don't really know how the body knows when to start this process, but it is as if there is a time clock in the brain that switches on the puberty process at a certain age. We know a lot about things that can affect this time clock, and particularly those that slow it down, and these were discussed on page 8.

THE TESTES GROW FIRST

The very first thing that happens in a boy who is starting puberty is the enlargement of his testes. This probably won't be noticed by the boy himself. It's a very gradual process, and the testes are quite small before puberty — only 2 or 3 mL in volume, and not much good for anything you might think. Actually they do make a small amount of hormone, and it is this hormone, made in early foetal life before birth, that has led to the development of the boy's penis and other male characteristics.

At the start of puberty, the testes increase in size from 3 mL in volume to 4 mL. At that time they start making more of the hormone called testosterone. It is this hormone that is responsible for many of the physical changes of puberty that will follow. The hormone also affects psychological changes, so we will hear more about it later on.

Over the next few years the testes will continue growing in size until they reach adult volume of 20 to 25 mL each. In the growing period it is generally true that the bigger they are, the more testosterone they are making. When they reach a certain size they will also be making sperm. Many of the landmarks of a boy's puberty, such as his first ejaculation of semen, his growth spurt and his voice break, can be related to the development of the testes. For this reason specialist doctors, when they are checking on growth and development, may need to estimate the volume of the testes. It is usual to measure them by comparing them with a set of graduated plastic or wooden testis models to check which one they match up with.

THE TESTES HANG LOWER IN THEIR POUCH

The testes are contained in a pouch or sac that is called the scrotum. At puberty the scrotum changes and becomes somewhat wrinkled in appearance. It enlarges to allow the testes to hang lower in hot weather. This is quite important, as it helps the testes to remain a little cooler than the rest of the body. The testes need to be a little cooler to preserve sperm and to remain healthy. There is a muscle to draw the testes up close to the body in cold weather to keep them warm. This also helps to protect them from injury.

PUBIC HAIR USUALLY STARTS TO APPEAR NEXT

Pubic hair is usually the first sign that the boy notices about himself as a start of puberty. The stimulus to start this hair growth usually comes from a different gland: the adrenal gland. This gland sits on top of the kidney. Occasionally it starts making hormones to produce pubic hair well in advance of the other stages of puberty, but more often this occurs some time after the testes have started to grow.

There is usually a small growth of fine, straight hairs at the base of the penis to start with. Gradually the area covered by hair extends over the pubic region and the hairs become thicker and later curly. At the very end of puberty, hair grows backwards between the boy's legs, down the thighs, and upwards in a line to the navel. The development of pubic hair can be a helpful sign to tell us how puberty is progressing, particularly as other aspects of puberty can relate to the stage of pubic hair that has been reached.

Later on still, hair develops on other parts of the body. Hair develops under the armpits fairly soon after the pubic hair has started to thicken. Hair on the face is usually on the upper lip initially, later appearing on the beard area of the chin and neck. Growth

of hair in front of the ears, in the sideburns area, is relatively late in puberty.

It is somewhat of a landmark in puberty when a young man starts shaving. Although it is a bit of a nuisance, it is a sign of maturity. The amount of body hair varies a lot between one boy and another. It is not a sign of virility: many strong men and some racial groups have a relatively small amount of body hair.

While we are on the subject of hair, hair on the front of the head may start to recede in some young men in their early twenties. This is also under the influence of the hormone testosterone.

THE PENIS STARTS TO GROW NEXT

Some time after the testes have started to enlarge, they will be making enough testosterone to stimulate the penis to grow. Some boys may be worried that they are still underdeveloped even though other signs of puberty are obvious. They just have to be patient: the penis sometimes takes its time to grow. You can't tell by the size of the penis before puberty how large it will become when it is fully developed.

At first the penis becomes longer. Later it increases in width. The boy will notice that it often becomes erect, and not always when it is convenient.

While all this is going on, glands inside the body, called the prostate gland and the seminal vesicles, are also growing under the influence of the hormone testosterone. The boy will be quite unaware of these developments, but these glands store sperm and make the liquid in which sperm can be carried out of the body. This liquid is called semen. Semen contains sperm, which has been stored in these glands ready for the boy to ejaculate from time to time.

SPERM AND EJACULATION

When the penis is fairly well developed, the pubic hair well formed and the testes are about 12 mL in size, the boy will have his first ejaculation of semen. In some ways this first ejaculation is like a girl's first period.

Certainly it is a landmark in sexual maturity and an indication that the boy is getting close to being able to father a child. Unlike a girl's first period, however, a boy usually keeps this event to himself, and may be quite embarrassed about it.

By the time a boy has his first ejaculation, he is making a lot of sperm. Unlike the girl, who has all her ova present (in an immature form) by the start of puberty, boys are making sperm throughout their adult life. The testicles are capable of making 50,000 sperm a minute. They can do this constantly from puberty onwards. It is not surprising that boys need to ejaculate them from time to time, either during sleep or by masturbation.

Masturbation can't waste sperm: there is a constantly renewed supply, day and night. (Masturbation is discussed in Chapter 7.)

GROWTH RATE INCREASES

Towards the end of early childhood and before puberty starts, the rate of growth in height slows down. At this stage a boy may only grow at the rate of 4 to 6 cm a year. Growth does not increase much in the early stages of puberty, but the rate steadily increases as puberty advances. When the testes are about halfway developed, and there is some development of pubic hair, the rate of growth in height increases greatly, perhaps up to 10 or 12 cm a year. This growth spurt is a rather late event in puberty in a boy, unlike a girl

(whose growth occurs early in puberty). It's hard for some boys who are late starters and who remain shorter than the girls in their year at school at a time when all the others are shooting up.

The first sign that growth is increasing is an increase in the size of the feet and hands. The boy may grow out of his shoes before he wears them out: new shoes that fitted well 6 months ago are now too tight.

Arms and legs start to grow later, at which stage height increases rapidly and the boy grows out of his clothes very quickly. He may seem all arms and legs and quite uncoordinated. This rapid change in his body needs some getting used to, and the boy may seem clumsy and gawky. Not for long. After the growth in legs and arms has slowed down, the spine goes on growing, and this may continue, rather slowly, until the young man is in his early twenties. This leads to adult body proportions and to the final adult height.

A further stage, and the last part of growing, is the development of the upper trunk, with broadening of the shoulders and strengthening of the bones. This leads to the final adult male body physique. Of course all bodies are a bit different and most of these differences are inherited from parents. Many boys are far from convinced that their body is perfect but they get used to it, and they become proud of it as their physique strengthens up and their muscles develop.

MUSCLE DEVELOPMENT FOLLOWS THE GROWTH SPURT

When a boy is growing rapidly, most of the body's effort is put into developing long and strong bones. At this time muscle development doesn't change much, and the boy is likely to be unimpressed with his muscles. Later in puberty, however, muscles do start to increase in size and in strength. This reaches a peak after growth has slowed down. It is at this stage that the boy will be most able to take part in competitive sports that require strength or do physical training that is designed to develop muscles and can safely embark on weights training, provided that it is properly supervised.

FAT STORES DIMINISH

While the body is growing rapidly, and later when his muscles are developing, the boy may lose some of his fat. This is most noticeable if he has been a little overweight. Like many of the other things that are going on during puberty, the increase in muscle development and loss of fat is under the influence of testosterone. The process is helped by the high levels of physical activity that many boys show at this age. It is much less marked in those boys who spend much of their time sitting around watching television or playing computer games.

THE VOICE BREAKS

The voice box (larynx) and vocal chords mature during puberty, and eventually the voice deepens as they increase in size and change in shape. While it is happening the boy may find that he doesn't have complete control of his voice — it may be quite deep one minute and then a high-pitched squeak emerges. The phrase 'the voice breaks' is a good one and describes it well. It occurs in mid to late puberty, and it can be a bit of a relief to some boys who may feel that they are likely to be treated as a child until they acquire an adult voice. In most boys, the voice is fully broken by the age of 16½ years.

OTHER CHANGES ARE HAPPENING TOO

While all this is happening, the skin changes, becoming more oily. This can lead to acne (discussed in Chapter 9). Pigmented moles may appear and old ones may increase in size; other moles may change in shape, and some may develop a pale 'halo' and eventually fade or disappear.

Body smell changes, and underarm sweating can become quite an embarrassment. Teenage boys have a definite and characteristic smell, which every mother recognizes, and is much worse if they leave their dirty clothes in a heap in their room for a few days.

Facial features change too. The nose changes from a little soft nose of a small child to the bony appearance of the adult; this is also affected by inherited factors, and many families are proud of their family nose.

Inside the face and skull, the sinuses are developing, and it is at this time that sinusitis may be a problem for some teenagers.

FINALLY THE BODY BECOMES THAT OF A MATURE MAN

All this process takes many years, and can become an agonizingly slow process for some boys, and bewilderingly quick for others. Most take it in their stride and watch their body mature with pleasure and delight.

When these physical changes are complete, we can say that puberty is complete. Some fine tuning will continue for a number of years, other changes will occur as a result of lifestyle or alterations in health. Most young men realize that although their own body may not be quite perfect, it is pretty good and something to be proud of and to look after.

Even though puberty may be complete, the process of adolescence may be far from over.

Puberty in a girl

THE PITUITARY GLAND STIMULATES THE OVARIES TO DEVELOP

The earliest changes of puberty pass unnoticed in a girl, as they are happening in her ovaries, tucked away in her pelvis. Even before this, the action which gets the whole process going is silently taking place in the pituitary gland. This gland is inside the head and just below the brain, and is responsible for coordinating growth and puberty.

At some time during a girl's mid-childhood, perhaps when she is 9 or 10 years old, the pituitary gland starts to send hormonal messages to the ovaries, signalling them to wake up and prepare for puberty. Until then the ovaries are quite

small, and although in early childhood they are quite capable of producing the female hormone oestrogen, they only do so in small amounts. Certainly they are quite unprepared for producing mature ova, even though all the immature ova cells are already formed.

The ovaries start to enlarge, and as they do, they produce oestrogen in small gland-like structures called follicles. This development can be shown on ultrasound, which gives a picture of what is going on inside the abdomen. An ultrasound would not, of course, be given unless there is a problem that needs sorting out (for instance, if there seemed to be an hormonal imbalance).

BREAST DEVELOPMENT IS USUALLY THE FIRST SIGN OF PUBERTY

As oestrogen is released into the bloodstream, it starts to produce the outward signs of puberty. The breasts start to enlarge, at first just under the nipples. Sometimes it starts on just one side (which may make a girl a bit worried) but the other side soon catches up. Often the developing breast feels a bit tender at first. Sometimes a mother is concerned that breast development has started when her daughter is so young: but it's a very early sign of puberty, and it may be quite a long time before the girl's periods start. Often the girl becomes very modest and self-conscious, and no-one in the house is allowed to see her undressed.

As puberty progresses, the breasts increase in size. The breast tissue, which started off just under the nipple area, extends in area. The initial nipple area remains rather prominent for some time, and only merges into the general contour of the breast at the end of puberty.

Some girls may feel that their breasts are less developed than other girls. There is, of course, great variation in what is normal. Whatever the girl may think about her breast development, small size does not make her any less able to breast-feed when it is time to have a baby, provided she is healthy.

PUBIC HAIR STARTS TO DEVELOP

About the same time that the breasts start to develop, or sometimes a little later (and sometimes a little before), pubic hair starts to grow. This hair is under the control of another hormone which is made, not in the ovaries, but in glands called the adrenal glands. The adrenal glands are receiving the same general message from the brain that determines that it is time for puberty, but this message comes through a different set of hormones. Oestrogen also stimulates hair development.

The first pubic hairs are not in the pubic region, but along the labia, which are the outer lips of the opening of the vagina. A little later, hair over the pubic region appears, and gradually extends in area and becomes thicker. The extent of this hair development, and the stage of breast development, tell us how puberty is progressing, and what should be happening in other parts of the body.

CHANGES INSIDE THE BODY

While these obvious signs of puberty are occurring, the girl's internal sexual development is also taking place. Her ovaries are enlarging and developing follicles that will in time be capable of releasing ova. Her vagina is enlarging, and under the influence of oestrogen, is producing increased amounts of mucus which has a different chemical composition than before. She may make quite a large volume of this mucus, and may worry that she has developed a discharge which is not healthy. In fact the mucus helps protect her internal sexual organs from infection, and is quite normal.

Her uterus (womb) is also developing in size and shape, and as she produces increasing amounts of oestrogen, the lining of her uterus thickens and develops a rich blood supply to prepare for future pregnancy.

It will still be some time before she has her first period. There are other changes to her body that must take place first.

THE GROWTH SPURT IS EARLY IN PUBERTY

Quite early in puberty, the girl will start to grow more rapidly. Her feet grow first and, soon after, her legs and arms. As puberty usually starts a bit earlier in girls than boys, and as the growth spurt in boys tends to be later in puberty, many girls are taller than many boys of their same age at this stage (boys soon catch up). Just before puberty, a girl may grow only 4 cm in a year, but once puberty is under way, her growth rate may increase to 9 or 10 cm a year. A few girls, already tall in early childhood, really shoot up at this time, and may seem to be heading for 6 feet (183 cm).

GIRLS USUALLY PUT ON WEIGHT (FAT) AT THIS STAGE

At the same stage of puberty, and as oestrogen levels in the blood rise, girls tend to put on a bit of weight. This is both natural and necessary for normal development. Some of the weight, which includes fat tissues beneath the skin, tends to be in the breast area, on the buttocks, upper thighs and lower part of the abdomen. This is sometimes referred to as the 'female distribution of fat', as it is, to a greater or lesser extent, universal amongst normal girls at this age. Even though it is normal, most girls don't like it, particularly when they compare their body with slim young women who have been specially chosen by magazines as models.

BODY SHAPE CHANGES

As puberty progresses, the general shape of the body changes. This is largely due to the way the bone structure is maturing, and particularly the pelvis, which increases in size. The bones of the pelvis guard the uterus and bladder, and provide a circle of bone around the lower abdomen. This is where the baby will emerge at childbirth, and it needs to be large enough for the baby's head to fit through.

Some girls feel that their body shape isn't as they would like, particularly their broad hips. It is just the result of this normal development of the pelvic bones, of course, and is a sign of becoming a mature woman.

BODY HAIR AND OILY SKIN

Later in puberty, the girl develops body hair. This varies a lot between one woman and another. It includes hair in the armpits and on the legs and arms. Some girls feel that they have developed excessive hair, and if so it is quite reasonable to ask for medical advice: sometimes, just occasionally, it is due to an hormonal imbalance which can be corrected.

Like boys, girls develop increased oiliness of the skin, especially on the face and chest. It is usually less marked than boys, but it can still lead to acne. In some girls the acne can be particularly severe during menstrual periods, and special hormonal treatment can sometimes help with this. (Acne is discussed in Chapter 9.)

MENARCHE: THE FIRST MENSTRUAL PERIOD

Towards the end of puberty, when the physical changes are nearing completion, and some 2 to 4 years after the breasts started to develop, menstrual periods start.

The start of menstruation is called menarche, and is the sign that sexual development is nearly complete. Menarche occurs when the rate of growth in height is slowing down. The girl can expect to grow for a bit longer, and perhaps another 5 or 6 cm or so. Most of her growth is complete,

however, except for further broadening of the skeleton and maturing of the body shape. Some growth of her spine continues.

Menarche usually occurs before the ovaries start to release ova. Sometimes this follows soon after, sometimes it may be delayed for a year or so. The girl cannot assume that she couldn't become pregnant at this stage: many girls are ovulating at or soon after their first period.

Menstrual periods are often erratic at first and there may be quite a long gap between the first and second period, even as long as 6 to 12 months. This is quite normal.

WHEN IS A GIRL ABLE TO REPRODUCE?

In childhood, the girl's ovaries contain about 400,000 undeveloped egg cells. These lie dormant until puberty. After the girl starts to menstruate, some of these will ultimately develop into mature ova, capable of starting a new life.

The average age for a girl to start menstruating is just before her thirteenth birthday. This also means that almost half the number of girls haven't had their first period by then, but at age 15, over 90% will be menstruating. Usually the first few periods are erratic, and there may be quite long intervals between periods. At this time it is likely that the girl will not be ovulating. Ovulation usually starts within a few months of the first period however. Some girls do ovulate at their first period, so it would be wrong to assume that girls can't become pregnant then.

CHAPTER 2

SELF-IDENTITY

Psychological and social changes at adolescence

Most parents of young children approaching puberty dread the emotional swings, the rebelliousness and general risky and thoughtless behaviour that is supposed to characterize adolescence. It is certainly true that a lot of emotional changes are taking place, and it is obvious that teenagers do have to move out into the wider world of their own age group, with all the attendant new experiences and challenges.

But it is not true that this period has to be a fearful and worrying time for parents. It is not true that parents lose all their influence in helping their child develop into a mature adult. Some children (and their parents) do have problems and difficulties along the way, but most do not. Most of those children who do have major difficulties will eventually emerge from their turbulent teenage years and mature into independent and reasonably sensible adults. If parents can survive this challenging time of their child's life, it will usually lead to a new and satisfying relationship with their young adult son or daughter. And even if the boy or girl did seem to reject his or her family's standards of behaviour as an adolescent, adulthood often heralds a return to family values.

WHY ALL THE EMOTIONAL HASSLE?

Why does adolescence involve so much emotional hassle for both child and parents? There are two sorts of answers to this question. The first and most obvious one is that it is all due to hormones.

The sex hormones of puberty not only cause the physical changes of adolescence, they also affect the mind and the emotions. Testosterone in the boy and oestrogen in the girl have a profound effect on how they feel. Women may recall their experiences and emotions during their own puberty to understand the effects that hormones have on their daughter. It is also true for testosterone, the male sex hormone. We know that boys who are given testosterone treatment because they have not yet entered puberty show all the emotional changes associated with puberty.

But there is another sort of answer. Our modern society is at odds with nature, and teenagers are the main victims. The natural process of adolescence has made them ready for physical work, their brain is ready for them to take responsibility for themselves and others, and their body is ready for sexual reproduction. This was fine before modern society demanded that children remain dependent long beyond puberty. Through the process of social and economic change, and in earlier societies before industrialization, children entered adult life rather abruptly when they were about 13 years old, and often through an initiation ceremony which marked the transition. Then they took on an adult role at once. There was no such thing as adolescence in those days. You were either a child or an adult. If you were a child, you were looked after. If you were an adult, you took on responsibilities for others, and were an equal amongst adults.

Now adolescents have to stay on at school to get further education. Teenagers have a lot of problems if they decide to have children in our society, even though sexually they are perfectly capable of doing so. Adolescents aren't expected to support their family by work now. Adolescents therefore remain dependent to some extent on others

for many years. They are living at home much longer. The average age for an American to leave home, for instance, is now in their mid twenties.

All this prolongs the period between childhood and adulthood. It was only in this century that we identified this period, and

gave it the name 'adolescence'. It is therefore more a psychological and social description than a physical one.

The fact that this period of life has been artificially created and prolonged by modern society accounts for many of the problems for teenagers and their families. These problems have been well recognized in Western society since the early twentieth century. They are now becoming increasingly manifest in the developing world.

One thing we have learnt about adolescence this century is the developmental process that they have to go through if they are to make a successful transition to adult life. The process can be described as having four main parts: becoming independent, seeking self-identity, sexuality, and finding their place in society.

BECOMING INDEPENDENT

No-one is absolutely independent — we all depend a bit on each other — but if we are to become responsible for ourselves, we must first reduce our dependence on our parents. This is the first step in leaving home, which may not take place until many years later. It isn't always an easy process, particularly if our parents aren't too keen to let us go in case we make bad mistakes.

If you were a teenager, you might start by challenging your parents' decisions about what you should do. You might argue with them about things that concern you. You might want more freedom to do the things you want. You might think it is time to find out about life by trying things out, by experimenting. You might check out how other teenagers behave and try out their style of behaviour instead of that of your parents.

In doing this you might go too far. You might make mistakes, even quite bad ones that could cause you harm. Your parents would want to protect you from this, but they may not be able to do so. So you might cause them a lot of worry, particularly if they still think of you as a dependent child, their responsibility.

SEEKING SELF-IDENTITY

As a child, you think of yourself as part of your family. As an adolescent, you start asking yourself: 'Who am I really — as a person, separate from my family?' This is an important part of growing up, of the process of separation and independence.

To find out more, teenagers tend to compare themselves with their own age group, their peers. They want to identify themselves with people outside their family: other teenagers, adults they admire, personalities on TV, sporting stars, or rock-group singers. In doing this comparison they may find they don't match up so well. Their family will probably come out even worse. This may be painful for them. It may take hours of talking to their friends, discussing their own inadequacies and that of their parents and their friends. It might take some boasting of their imagined or real achievements. It might mean doing things to impress others even if they feel it probably isn't right. It might mean getting rather depressed about themselves. It might, for a few, mean trying to make changes in themselves that are inappropriate, such as dieting to excess, dyeing their hair a strange colour, body piercing, or tattooing.

SEXUALITY

Some people are a little jealous of teenagers' sexual opportunities and capacity. There is no doubt that their awakening sexual arousal, their increasing sexual ability, and the attractiveness of youth for each other, all occupy a great deal of most teenagers' time and thoughts. The trouble is that nature has provided them with all this sexual urge and ability, but reproduction is not yet socially appropriate. Most teenagers work it out for themselves, particularly as society has given them much more information about sex and much more freedom to try it out safely.

There are still the problems of sexual identity. Of accepting themselves as sexual beings, with sexual interests and drives that may be disturbing, particularly if there are feelings about homosexuality. (This is discussed more in Chapter 7.)

The final stage of sexual development is when it becomes part of the intimacy of a personal relationship. Sex is a sensation, and current magazines spend a lot of time explaining how to make it better for both partners. Sex also provides an intimate closeness that, for the mature adolescent, may allow fulfilment of their relationship with another person.

A PLACE IN SOCIETY

The final developmental process of adolescence looks into the future. If the first stage asks: 'What can I do by myself?'; and the second stage asks: 'Who am I as an individual?'; the third stage asks: 'What will I be?'. This involves determining a career in life. What job will they do? How will they fit into society? Where do they feel their responsibilities to other people lie?

With the competition for places in tertiary education, and the high unemployment rate for young people, this stage is often confusing for teenagers. It was a lot easier when boys expected to go into their father's craft or business, and girls were expected to become wives like their mothers. Those days have gone — and a good thing too, no doubt — but not without a heavy price for many teenagers whose future place in society remains in doubt for them for many years.

WHAT CAN PARENTS DO TO HELP?

Just be around and support them when they need it. Understand their difficulties and their mistakes. Teenagers have to go through this process of development themselves. It is our present society's substitute for the initiation ceremony of the past. It is painful for teenagers, but most take it in their stride. It is a worry for many parents, as they watch their teenager try things out, make wrong decisions and do risky things. It's just as well that parents don't know half the things their teenager gets up to.

All this means is that it is better that teenagers go through adolescence at their own pace and make their own running. Parents shouldn't try to protect them from all the hazards of this age, partly because they couldn't, partly because it's a personal process that teenagers really have to work out for themselves, and partly because if they don't go through adolescence in the teenage years, there may be many more serious troubles for them when they are older.

It's not good to be a retarded adolescent when you are an adult. You might be unreliable and not fulfil your responsibilities. You might have trouble sustaining a long-term relationship. You might be self-centred and selfish. You might get stuck on drugs instead of just trying them out briefly with your friends.

Don't despair

One more thing. Adolescence is a very interesting time for parents. Adolescents are more interesting to talk to, more challenging to argue with, more fun to play with. They might beat you at games. They would be more useful if you go camping together. They might catch fish if you go fishing. They might baby sit and help with the shopping. It's never dull with teenagers in the house and the rewards for helping them through their own personal developments are great.

How teenagers think

A group of teenagers was talking about drinking at a party. The problem was that some of them were going to be driving home. Should they risk having a few drinks? Everyone else was. This is the way that some of them looked at it.

Gary: 'You'd be stupid to drink and then drive because if you did you might get breathalysed and lose your licence. It's safe round where we live though, because there aren't any booze buses there.'

Jane: 'You shouldn't drink and then drive because alcohol affects your brain, and if alcohol gets to a certain level in your blood it could affect your judgment and slow down your reflexes in a crisis on the road.'

Wayne: 'What they say about alcohol slowing down your brain is just trying to put you off drinking. It doesn't happen to me. I can drink six stubbies in a night and feel fine.'

Sometimes you would have to be a genius to know how teenagers think. They don't seem to listen to reason. They don't think ahead. They hear you alright but don't seem to pay any attention. They are smart but they don't show it in their behaviour. You can talk to them for hours and it goes in one ear and out the other. You give them good advice and they just accuse you of nagging. Or of being old fashioned. 'Yeah yeah, I know, "Back in my day, when I was your age . . ."' They even mock you when you are trying to be helpful and wanting to save them from making the mistakes you made.

Actually we do know quite a lot about how teenagers *can* think. But sometimes we expect too much of them. Just because they are getting big and acting cool, it doesn't mean that they are ready to think logically and in a mature way. And sometimes there are other things on their mind, personal problems or stress at school perhaps, which get in the way of thinking properly or acting sensibly. And of course, you can't lump all teenagers together. They vary in how well they can think (as do young children and adults — everyone has different abilities).

Perhaps the most infuriating thing about teenagers and the way they think is their capacity to think rationally and sensibly one day, and like complete idiots the next.

THE BRAIN BECOMES MORE MATURE THROUGH ADOLESCENCE

Even taking all this into account, as children reach maturity they do develop mature ways of thinking. Although most, if not all, of a person's brain cells are developed in infancy, and although the brain has almost completed growth in size before puberty starts, the way the brain functions does change in very important ways during adolescence. It becomes capable of logical thought. It can examine beliefs and information that have been taken for granted during childhood.

There is a difference between (a) learning facts and gaining information (which is what children are doing every day from infancy), and (b) linking these pieces of information and facts into logical thought (which is essentially an adult form of thinking).

In primary school, and in daily living, young children are absorbing a great deal of knowledge. They will also develop a whole system of beliefs, some of which will be based on things they see around them, some on things they hear from their families and from teachers, and some they read or see on television. Some things (like religious belief), children accept because they have been told these things by people they trust.

It is usually impossible for young children to know the difference between information that is based on fact and that which is fantasy, prejudice or just a guess. Sometimes they have clues of course: if it's in a comic, it's fantasy. If your parents tell you, it's fact. If it's on television, you aren't sure. If it comes from someone you don't like, you may not accept it at all. But whatever way young children acquire information and develop beliefs, it will be very hard for them to link these pieces of information together and to apply them to new situations. This is sometimes called abstract thinking, or conceptual thinking, and it is this kind of thinking that develops during adolescence. It's the basis for much of learning in secondary school, and if teenagers have difficulty in this way of thinking, secondary school may be quite difficult for them.

TEENAGERS START TO QUESTION THEIR BELIEFS

During adolescence, and as they acquire this more complex form of thinking, children are more able to question beliefs that they had previously taken for granted because someone they trusted had told them these things were fact.

As they are trying to become more independent from their parents in their daily life, so they tend to become more independent in their thinking. This can be very disconcerting for parents who feel that their teenager is throwing away all the family values in the process. Perhaps their teenager is challenging family religious beliefs. Perhaps the teenager is telling his or her parents that they are basically stupid.

All this is very upsetting for parents, but take heart. Most young people come back to family values as they grow up, and most come to realize that their parents weren't as stupid as they thought (or maybe their parents learnt a lot in the last few years).

THEY DON'T LISTEN IF THEY ARE LOOKING AT SOMETHING ELSE

Teenagers (and perhaps this is true for all ages) have difficulty in listening to anything when their attention is on something else. If they are watching television, they won't hear you call them to set the table or wash their hands or feed the dog. You can shout and they can make some kind of noise that makes you think that they have heard, but they haven't really. And afterwards when you are really mad with them for not doing what you asked, they claim you only asked once, and they have the nerve to ask you to stop nagging.

If you want your teenager to listen to you, you will have to make them look at you. You may have to put yourself between the teenager and the soapie on television. After their yells have died down, they will probably hear what you have to say. Most mothers know this well: 'Look at me when I am speaking to you' isn't just asking for politeness, it is to ensure that the teenager's mind isn't on something else. Most people will have had the experience of listening to the radio while they are driving, and then, after they have negotiated some road crisis, realizing that they haven't heard anything.

FATHER TO DAUGHTER... ARE YOU RECEIVING ME?

THEY DON'T THINK BEFORE THEY ACT

It would be so easy if teenage behaviour were governed by rational thought, and if teenagers considered the long-term consequences of their actions before doing silly and risky things that they know perfectly well they shouldn't. It isn't that they are stupid: they just do stupid things without thinking sometimes.

Some parents think that teenagers do stupid things all the time without thinking. No matter how often you give advice, they forget it, and maybe do the opposite to what you suggest. Is this because they are not thinking? Is it because they are trying to break away from parental control? Are they just trying to annoy you by challenging your authority? Are they incapable of logical thought?

One way to resolve these questions is to look at how your teenager is coping with learning at school. A teenager who is doing competent work can't be dumb.

How do you get on together? If there is a lot of conflict, perhaps your teenager is showing independence by not listening to you and your advice. Perhaps there are other things on your teenager's mind that get in the way of sensible thinking just at present.

When all else fails, it is best not to rely on logical explanation alone when telling things to teenagers. You may need to give firm advice (with explanation) and tell them the immediate consequences of not following it ('You will be grounded' or 'You won't get to use the car'), rather than hypothetical discussions of long-term possible outcomes.

Coming back to the teenagers who were thinking about drinking and driving. Their conversation showed the ability of rational thought (Jane), of immature thought limited to immediate consequences (Gary), and of irrational belief (Wayne). Yet in a way, all were right. The main fear for teenagers is to lose their driver's licence, and that's why they usually don't drink and then drive. Adults often think the same way. Jane is the logical one, but Wayne is probably quite right in thinking people are trying to stop him drinking by threatening him.

Risky things that teenagers do

'Our parents don't know what we're doing half the time. If they did they'd die. Or kill us. It's just as well they don't know, then they don't worry. We're all right though. They needn't worry.'

Teenagers have the reputation of taking risks that may endanger their health, their safety, the safety of others, their future and even their lives.

But we all take risks throughout our lives. Perhaps not so many as we grow older and more responsible or more anxious. We may take risks when driving in a hurry. We may take financial risks, or risks in career decisions. We take risks if we smoke, eat too much, drink too much. Some people may say that we take risks when we marry or take on a life partner. Certainly we take risks when we decide to have a child.

Young children take risks too. Toddlers climb, poke keys into power points, fall into swimming pools, drink poisons and do many other awful things when they get half a chance. Older children run onto the road, climb trees, and ride skateboards. So what's so different about teenagers?

Teenagers tend to take risks in the same way as younger children, but with less restraining influences. They are not so worried as to what their parents or teacher may think or do. They may still, like children, fail to think ahead about the possible consequences. In that way they differ from adults, who tend to take calculated risks.

Teenagers have much more opportunity than children to do risky things. They are much less supervised, much more mobile, much better at working out ways of not getting caught. Many have more time on their hands, and greater capacity to get bored. Doing something that is risky is a great recipe to beat boredom.

Teenagers, like children but more so, like to try things out for themselves. To experiment.

What does it feel like to smoke cigarettes? To sniff chrome? To smoke dope? To get drunk? To drive a car fast? To have sex? To have green hair? It can't be that serious, considering that everyone else does it. If you always obeyed your parents you'd never have fun or learn anything about the real world. Anyway they probably tried it themselves when they were young, and they survived. You wouldn't be here at all if they hadn't tried sex.

TEENAGERS LIKE TO DO THINGS TOGETHER AND BE LIKE EACH OTHER

Another thing: teenagers are under a lot of pressure to be like their friends, and to do the things that they do (or what they think their friends do). The pressure may not necessarily come from their friends, but from within themselves to meet the expectations of their friends, and to be part of the group.

The problem for parents is that teenagers have the capacity to take great risks, but haven't yet developed the maturity to consider the full consequences. They have immense energy for things they enjoy or that excite them. Pity they haven't the same

energy for household chores, and boring and useful things like that.

Parents don't always know exactly what their teenager is up to, and sometimes it is better, for their own peace of mind, not to know. But if they do find out that their teenager has done something risky, or against their advice and wishes, it may be helpful to know what other teenagers in the community are doing. It may not condone their child's actions, or excuse them, but it may help to put things into perspective.

The statistics quoted in this book about sexual behaviour, drugs, smoking and alcohol have come from major surveys of Australian children and adolescents, and have been published in reports and professional journals (listed at the back of the book). To some people the statistics may seem hard to believe. Of course just because many teenagers do something, it does not mean that a particular teenager or a particular group of teenagers do it.

You can look at statistics two ways. If 30% of 15 year olds smoke, you could say, quite properly: 'That's awful, something has to be done about it.' Or you could say: 'That means that 70% don't smoke. That's great. They resist all that peer pressure and think about their health in a responsible way.'

Self-esteem: feeling good about yourself

'He's got very low self-esteem, doctor. He feels bad about himself. He doesn't think he's any good at sport (well he isn't really, but at least he used to try). We tell him he could look quite nice if he held himself properly, but he doesn't believe us. He says he's no good at school, but if he worked hard I am sure he'd get a pass in his year.'

Michael looked pretty miserable as he heard this series of put-downs. His mother was seeking help to make him feel better about himself, but was probably reinforcing his feeling of worthlessness.

Children get a sense about themselves, and their value, when they are quite young. This largely comes from their parents — parents who are very proud of their children, proud of their parenthood, of the small human beings they created. It is this sense of being valuable that leads to young children feeling good about themselves. The value stems initially from the love that parents feel for their children. It is enhanced with every new achievement their children make, such as the first steps, the first words, the ability to dress themselves, the first day at school, the first school report, the first netball game . . .

It is these repeated expressions of pride from parents that lead to children's development of self-esteem. This feeling of self-worth will be reinforced through childhood and should stand them in good stead as they enter the stage of adolescence when they start to question their parents' viewpoint and their own sense of identity.

Self-worth may take a bit of a battering when the child goes to school, and gets teased by others or put down by a harassed teacher. It may be threatened by the presence of an older brother who has already done everything, who learned to speak earlier, ran at an earlier age, and is now reading books and playing football and given extra pocket money and liked better by his grandparents because he was the first grandchild.

Of course all this may be just the child's impression of their parents' feelings for each member of the family. But children tend to be very perceptive: another child in the family may really be smarter, better natured or better at sport. Although parents may often say that they love all their children and treat them the same, children know that they don't get treated the same as each other (they couldn't, as no family could possibly treat each child the same). Children get firm impressions of where they stand in their parents' estimation, and this does not just depend on being loved.

Children start to decide how smart they are, and how valued they are, by the age of 9 or 10. It is then that they may become vulnerable to feelings of self-doubt, just when they are about to embark on puberty.

Once teenagers are in adolescence, their self-esteem takes on a new vulnerability: what other teenagers think of them may become even more important than what their parents think of them. They are competing for recognition. They want to be valued amongst their group. They want someone to want to sit next to them, to eat lunch with them. They want to be respected by their peers.

Much of this struggle for identity and acceptance by peers passes unnoticed by parents. If, however, a young teenager does have a problem, and is not meeting their parents' expectations and hopes, parents have a dilemma. Should they make their disappointment clear to their child, in the hope that they will improve? Yet if they do, it might be devastating to their teenager, who may be experiencing difficulties enough at school.

DOES SELF-ESTEEM REALLY MATTER?

Yes, it matters a great deal. Teenagers with poor self-esteem tend to be miserable, feel worthless and become depressed. They are liable to underachieve at whatever they do, and to have difficulty making friends. They are more likely to get into the wrong group of teenagers who also underachieve, and get their satisfaction within that group. If they do this, they are more likely to abuse drugs and alcohol, more likely to wag school, or drop out altogether. The social problems that follow may involve trouble with the police.

PARENTS NEED TO BE PROUD OF THEIR TEENAGER — LOVE IS NOT ENOUGH FOR AN ADOLESCENT

'Yeah, well, I know they love me — they have to, don't they? But they are always putting me down. I can't do anything right. I know I'm not much good at football, but Dad didn't even come to watch me play when I got picked for the first time to play in a match last week. They are always on about how good Robert is. They take him to basketball every week, you should hear them

OH SHE DID SO WELL ○ ○ ○ ○ ○
IN THE TOP 5% OF THE STATE!

boasting about him to all their friends.'

Geoffrey was sounding off about his parents, and he seemed to have a point. They claimed that there wasn't much they could do for him. He didn't seem interested in being taken to sport to watch his brother play. He was always being grounded, anyway, for bad behaviour and smoking.

Teenagers are very sensitive about what their parents and everyone else thinks about them. Parents are still the most important people in the early teenage years. It is not enough to be guiding teenagers through their mistakes and failings in these years. It is necessary to respect them and to be proud of them. There may not seem much to be proud about, but all children and teenagers have some things that are remarkable and good.

PRAISE CAN BE A PUT-DOWN: A FOR EFFORT, F FOR ACHIEVEMENT

Being proud about your teenager is not the same as praising them. It is very important to acknowledge a teenager's achievements, of course, but some parents tend to praise their child just for effort, rather than achievement. Maybe little children like this, but most teenagers really hate being praised for achieving something that they have done with great effort, but which everyone else can do with little effort. It's a bit of a put-down. It is especially annoying if their achievement isn't all that outstanding anyway.

Parents should think about what their teenager can do well and without too much effort. Is it art? Is it woodwork, or drama or gardening or fixing things? Whatever it is, that is what he or she wants recognition for.

PARENTS SHOULD BOAST ABOUT THEIR TEENAGER

The thing that really helps teenagers preserve self-esteem is knowing that their parents boast about them amongst their friends. It should be done repeatedly, and in their teenager's hearing, even if their friends might get bored hearing it. Parents tend to go on about their babies without worrying too much if they are boring their friends. Teenagers are much more interesting to other people than babies, who only really interest their parents and grandparents.

Surviving misfortune: the resilience of youth

Mrs Jones and her son Peter were discussing with me how well he had coped with his diabetes. He had developed diabetes when he was 12, and since then had given himself two shots of insulin every day, had two or three finger pricks each day to measure the level of sugar in his blood, and had to watch what he ate all the time. Now, at the age of 14, he seemed a perfectly normal teenager, coping well at school and with a good social life.

I was particularly interested, because just a little earlier, I had been listening to a girl of the same age who told me how much her diabetes had ruined her life. She found that having a chronic disease and the heavy demands of its treatment too much for her. As a result she always felt unwell and was also failing at school and had dropped out of netball, which she used to enjoy.

What is it that makes one young person cope well with adversity, while another hardly copes at all? Why does one girl take her asthma-prevention treatment regularly, while another constantly 'forgets' and consequently has one attack of asthma after another? How is it that when a marriage fails, and parents separate, one child may become emotionally disturbed and show distressing behaviour, while another seems to be taking it quite well?

Why does one youth get into drugs, while another may try them, but decide not to use them regularly, even though many of his friends do so? Why does one teenager drop out of school, even though she is quite bright, while another, with similar potential, stays at school and goes on to tertiary education?

There is no general answer to all these questions, of course. People are different, circumstances are different, and personalities are different; perhaps some people have the support they need, while others don't.

Parents do want to protect their teenager from life's adversities as much as possible. They know that they can't fully protect their child from all the bad things they will meet, but they hope that when their teenager encounters misfortune or personal risk, they will have the strength to overcome it.

HOW CAN YOU PROTECT YOUR TEENAGER?

You can approach this in two ways. The first is to minimize the risks that teenagers run into in their daily life: the difficulties that they may encounter at school, through friends and the world at large. The second is to help teenagers develop inner strengths that will enable them to resist those risks that they will inevitably encounter.

MINIMIZING THE RISKS

You can try to help your teenager avoid risks to his or her health and happiness, in the same way that you would put a fence around a backyard swimming pool to protect a toddler from falling in.

You might send your teenager to a school that has a good reputation for pastoral care and a sound curriculum, as school plays a very important part in

influencing teen behaviour. You can set a good example by not smoking — teenagers are much more likely to smoke if one or other parent smokes — and by not drinking to excess. You can make sure that you know where your teenager is at all times, and who their friends are. You can make sure that they know all about the hazards of risky behaviour such as taking drugs and having unprotected sex.

YOU CAN HELP DEVELOP YOUR TEENAGER'S PERSONAL STRENGTHS

It is important to minimize risks but, life being what it is in a modern urban society, your teenager can't avoid them completely. And you can't always predict misfortune. So the other way to protect your teenager is to give him or her the strengths to withstand adversity. This is sometimes referred to as *resilience*.

We know that most teenagers are very resilient. That is to say, they bounce back from adversity, rather than giving in to it. They resist temptation to damage their lives, even though there are plenty of very attractive opportunities all around them. They survive and even gain strength from problems through overcoming them.

TEENAGERS NEED A FIRM BASE: THEY NEED TO BELONG

Make sure that your teenager feels that he or she belongs to the family. A sense of belonging is one of the most important things that parents can give their teenager.

Although the teenage years are a time when teenagers themselves start to loosen the ties of family in order to have an identity of their own, the family is still very important to them. And it is quite possible for a person to achieve some degree of independence while still feeling that they belong to their own family. So many teenagers feel that because they appear to be rejecting their parents, their parents are rejecting them.

It has been suggested that while teenagers

want to fly, and to fly high, they also need to know that there is familiar ground to land on when it is time to return to earth.

Teenagers, if they are lucky, can also get a sense of belonging to their school. In fact school life, as a source of friendship, as a pathway to a career, and as a resource of responsible adults for guidance, is second only in importance to family life. Schools have the responsibility of fostering this sense of belonging, and parents should encourage it. For some teenagers who do not have a stable home life, including those homeless youths who still go to school, belonging to that school may be of critical importance in helping them cope with life.

This need to belong is very real for teenagers. Some may join a youth group, a sporting club, or a church group. If they do, it gives them the opportunity to enhance this sense of belonging. This goes far beyond just going there or participating in a group's activities. It meets a very real need to belong — a need we all have, but never more than in teenage. The need to belong to a group accounts for the many teenage gangs that exist in large cities.

SHARED MISFORTUNE

If there are things going wrong for the family, it is important that all the children feel that they are sharing the problem together. If one parent is mentally ill, or alcoholic, the teenager should not feel that he or she is bearing most of the brunt of this, even though they may be the oldest, and perhaps the most responsible. If a parent is out of work, and money is tight, no member of the family should feel that they are making the greatest sacrifice.

HOLDING THE FORT WHEN THE FAMILY IS AT WAR

If there is constant family conflict, perhaps when one parent is aggressive or mentally ill or violent, a teenager will cope best if there is one parent who remains stable and understanding and supportive. This is asking rather a lot for some parents in some family situations. But if the children, particularly the teenager, feel that no-one can be trusted to act as a caring and supportive parent, they will not cope well.

TRY TO SEE CHANGE AS BENEFICIAL

It often adds to the stress of adolescence if there are many changes in a teenager's life. Moving house, changing schools, or a new step-mother or step-father, can all seem distressing to a teenager. It is helpful to emphasize the positive aspects of change, that is, the way the change will benefit your teenager.

MAKE SURE YOUR TEENAGER ENJOYS SUCCESS IN SOMETHING

No-one should be made to feel a complete failure. Everyone needs to feel that they are achieving some success in their lives. It may not be at schoolwork, or competitive sport. It may be in raising and caring for a pet. It may be in a hobby, or a craft, in art or photography or growing things in the garden. Many teenagers who can't do well at competitive sport do well at martial arts. Whatever it is, the teenager should feel good about his or her achievements, and be given plenty of enthusiastic praise.

ENHANCE SELF-ESTEEM

Teenagers need to feel good about themselves. They are more likely to feel good if people who are important to them think well of them. Despite all the arguments and fights that occur in any home where there are teenagers, it is the parents who matter most. The attitudes of parents and friends can boost self-esteem, in the same way that constant criticism eventually wears anyone down. Self-esteem is also enhanced by successful achievement, and by recognition of this achievement by parents.

Helping plan ahead

Resilience is helped when teenagers start planning ahead. If they don't know where they are going in life, or how they will cope if something goes wrong, they won't cope so well if something bad does happen, or when the pressure is on to make an important decision.

Parents can help their teenager plan ahead, or at least think of options. This is a time when young people don't do so well if they just drift.

CHAPTER 3

FAMILY, AND FAMILY RULES

Family relationships

Thirteen-year-old Garry was the centre of constant rows in his family. Home had become a battleground, with noisy and bitter fights between Garry and his older brother Dean.

The family decided that Dean had to leave home. Dean was 17, had left school, and everyone found him a pain. His mother had packed his bags, his father had told him to get out until he had got a job, and his sisters said that life would be much more peaceful without him. Dean made it clear that if that was the way they felt he may as well go. But he didn't really want to leave home yet and he felt abandoned by his family, who favoured his stupid brother Garry (who started the fights, anyway).

Teenagers often take their frustrations and bad moods out on their brothers and sisters. It leads to rows about silly things, and to remarks that are unnecessarily cruel. As the family seem to gang up on them, or parents blame them because they think they should know better and be more mature, teenagers may feel less and less part of their family.

TEENAGERS ARE STILL PART OF THE FAMILY

Some of the time, teenagers are trying to escape the ties of family life. Some of the time, their family annoys them as much as they annoy their family. At these times parents can't wait for their terrible teenager to leave them in peace. And the teenager says that they can't wait to leave home. Everyone agrees that relationships will probably improve when the teenager does leave home, and only comes back occasionally (and even then, only when they are in a better mood).

At other times (and this is really most of the time for most families) teenagers remain very much part of the family. They need the family for many things: shelter, food, warmth, a place to sleep and do homework. They need to play with the dog and make snacks when they are hungry. They need money and someone to wash their clothes. Above all they need to be loved and to belong. They need to know that however awful they have been, there is someone to forgive them and help them start afresh. They need support when the world seems against them. They need someone to sound off to when they are in a bad mood.

How could anyone, except their family, put up with all this? And even for them it takes a lot of patience and understanding. Relationships are likely to be strained. Fathers ask why they should put up with this when they come home from a hard day and need to relax. Fathers may provide most of the money for them, and the least the teenager could do is to obey the family rules and show some respect. Mothers may also work outside the home, and may provide money to support the teenager. In addition mothers get tired and could do with some help around the house and some peace. Siblings wonder how their older brother or sister can get away with so much bad behaviour and broken rules. It isn't fair. And everyone agrees that it sets a bad example.

Sometimes a belligerent teenage boy finds it very hard to maintain any kind of conversation with his father, and his father, who can't begin to see his son's viewpoint,

feels the same way. Teenage girls can be just as bad.

These are the bad times, which are fortunately few for most families. Most families cope one way or another with the rows and enjoy the good times when they come. But relationships can suffer. Sometimes one member of the family — often the mother, but sometimes the father or a sibling — is the main peace-keeper and works hard to protect other members of the family.

BROTHERS AND SISTERS OFTEN FIGHT

There is nothing new about teenage when it comes to fights between siblings. At this age fights can get quite rough, and brothers and sisters are really good at giving insults, so you may worry that they may hurt each other. They can certainly hurt each other's feelings.

How can you prevent these fights from becoming serious? How can you restore

family harmony when tempers are high?

The first question is to decide whether you should intervene at all. So long as brothers and sisters don't really look like hurting each other, it may be better to let them work it out for themselves. It's part of growing up, and you can patch hurt feelings and grievances later when tempers have cooled.

The worst thing may be the noise they make which disturbs everyone else in the family. In that case you may have to settle the argument by turning off the television, or execute rough justice by sending everyone off to their own room. Maybe you can give them a job to do helping you.

If the row threatens to end up with someone getting very upset, you will have to separate brothers and sisters for a while. Try not to take sides, even if you know that one of them was very much at fault. Perhaps the fight was over something trivial, but the teenager who started it has had a bad day at school and has brought his or her worries home.

You may need to find out why your teenager got so irritable and violent with a brother or sister. It will help if they feel that you have at least listened to their side of the argument. This will help your teenager to see your point of view and realize how their sibling may have felt too. They might even be prepared to apologize, or make amends by being nice to their brother or sister later in the day.

Sometimes it is reassuring both to yourself as a parent and to the other members of the family to put fights in perspective. For example, I sometimes ask teenage boys what they would do if they saw their young brother (whom they are horrible to at home) attacked by a group of people in the street. They almost always say that they would defend their brother, of course. By acknowledging this, they are acknowledging their better feelings, saying that siblings do stick up for one another when it's really serious. The younger sibling feels a bit better when he hears that his elder brother would defend him and doesn't really want him to be badly hurt.

SOMETIMES TWO SIBLINGS WILL GANG UP AGAINST A THIRD

It is quite common for children in a family to pair up. Maybe they get along because of age differences, or similar interests, or just compatible personalities. That's fine, but it may mean that someone gets left out.

In teenage that can lead to misery for the child who is left out, unless there are other things in the teenager's life that compensate for lack of sibling support. The teenager will probably cope if he or she is good at sport or has good friends. If not, parents may have to look at ways at making him or her feel part of the family. This might mean involving the teenager in activities with his or her siblings, or sometimes splitting up the pair for outings or jobs around the house. Make sure there are some special times that are just for the teenager, when you can talk about any difficulties that they may have. Don't show favouritism of course, or it may only separate the teenager further from their siblings.

Sometimes teenage children get a lot from talking about personal problems with an older brother or sister. If a younger child seems left out in sibling relationships, it may be good to give the teenager in the family the job of helping a younger sibling.

If fights between siblings are quite out of hand, and nothing you have tried seems to work, consider whether family therapy might help.

What about Garry and Dean? It was really Dean who needed some help. He felt he was being excluded from the family and was taking it out on Garry, who didn't have the maturity or the inner strengths to cope with constant harassment from an older brother whom he really wanted to admire. When Dean got some help with getting his own life in order, and when he was helped to plan for his eventual and (one would hope) peaceful separation from his family, things got much better for the whole family. And Garry asked Dean to take him to the football.

Mothers and daughters (and fathers)

'She's a teenager from hell.' Fiona's mother seemed almost proud of her awful daughter. 'She argues with everything I say, she stays out later than we agree. Just look at her hair! She smokes, and I suspect that that's not all.'

Fiona didn't look too put out by these revelations. She certainly seemed to be making a statement about herself, with streaks of green in her hair, some heavy jewellery on her ears and a neat stud in her nose. Fiona actually looked pretty good, in a horrible sort of way, and I complimented her on her clothes. I said that I quite liked her hair.

Considering Fiona had asked for the pill last time we had met (when she hadn't allowed her mother into the room), I suspected that her mother had reason to feel insecure about her daughter, who was just 15. Fiona's mother thought that it was time to get down to taking her worries seriously.

'What really worries me is that we can't talk any more. Whatever happened to the little girl who was so close to me? She used to tell me everything.'

Mothers and daughters have a very special relationship. There are some things that it is awkward to talk about with fathers (or other males), such as breast development and buying a bra, and periods and what to do about them. Mothers can teach their teenage daughters about sexual things. Mothers can understand the hassles of relationships at school, and how hurtful other girls can be at times, and how really stupid and immature boys can be (except for this one guy . . .). Some mothers find difficulty in going beyond the basics of bras and periods, of course, and may miss the opportunity to help their daughter with her concerns about sexual feelings and relationships.

Fathers and daughters have a special relationship too, and it is different. A father has a unique responsibility to help his daughter develop trust in a man who cares for her. Fathers can help her to understand the complex differences of psychology and behaviour between men and women. They can help her feel that a man can respect a young woman, and care for her, as she can care for him. This trust is very precious, and very fragile. To break it is devastating.

A difficulty for some girls as they enter adolescence is that the close and sharing relationship that they have enjoyed with their mother can get in the way of loosening some of the ties of dependence on parents and developing a sense of self-identity. It will also be more difficult to maintain this close relationship while challenging family values and exploring the teenage world of adolescence.

Another thing. Teenagers, particularly girls, don't really like to hurt their mothers. If they told them about all their secret miseries and fears, it would be terribly upsetting for their mother. It is really better to discuss these deep personal matters with your friends. They actually enjoy hearing how miserable and worried you are. It's better to talk to someone who enjoys listening to you. If you told your mother, she would probably have a nervous breakdown, and then send you to a psychiatrist. That doesn't mean that you can't tell your mother that you hate her, and that you know that she hates you. That is really satisfactory to get a reaction, and of course she should know that you don't really mean it. (Or not all the time, anyway.)

There is no fail-safe way to get on with a daughter. Most mothers and daughters usually get along most of the time. If you don't get along with your daughter most of the time, it will be important to explore if there is something worrying her: at school, with friends, within the family, or with a particular friendship. Perhaps your daughter is taking it out on you, her mother. After all, who else is there to take it out on?

You can best help your daughter by staying around and being a firm base for her to come back to when she is ready or needs support. You don't need to lower family standards, but you should try not to be too judgmental, as your daughter may need to try things out for herself and make mistakes doing so.

What about Fiona, the teenager from hell?

Her mother and I agreed that ideally 15-year-old girls should be put in cold storage for a year or so. But as this wasn't practical, it might be better to suffer her moods and irrational behaviour and new-found reticence for a while. Fiona still needed protection and a solid family base from which to explore the world, and she would make mistakes.

But she was still the same daughter under the green hair and nose stud, and she would return to a good (but changed) relationship in time and with patience.

Fiona said of course she still loved her mother, she just wanted to be left alone sometimes. 'And don't worry so much. I'm not stupid, you know.'

Fathers and sons (and mothers)

I recently chanced to meet the mother of a boy who had been under my care two years before. At that time his behaviour was a great worry to everyone. He had dropped out of school, was having trouble with the police because he had stolen from neighbours' houses, was disagreeable to live with and argued violently with his sisters.

He came to my care because he had tried to kill himself. Fortunately he did no great harm to himself, and the attempt allowed his mother to consider what was troubling him so badly (rather than just dwelling on his bad behaviour).

His father was living in another state and had left all the responsibility of care of his children, including his difficult teenage son, to their mother. He didn't see them often, and when he did, he showed little interest in the boy. The old painful arguments between the parents would start again, usually around the father's apparent neglect of his family. Peter's mother said that Peter was turning out just like his father.

It became apparent to me, and to his mother, that Peter was really missing his father, and deeply hurt that he didn't seem interested in him. The police involvement, and then his attempted suicide, brought his father back into the picture.

I saw Peter and his father together while the boy was still in hospital. He looked just like his Dad, and sat close to him in my office. They joked a bit about things, and were discussing whether Peter could go to live with his father. If he did, it would be rather cramped. Peter would have to find a job. He'd have to help look after the flat. He'd have to obey house rules set by his father (who had got used to living alone).

Peter and his mother agreed to all this and I didn't see either of them again.

A TEENAGE BOY NEEDS HIS FATHER

Many teenage boys see little of their fathers. One family in four has split up by the time the children are adolescent, when the father is living away from the family. Sometimes a father works long hours, is tired when he comes home, and can't be bothered with his difficult and moody son. Some fathers have such high expectations of their children, their main contact is to reinforce the comments in school reports that 'he could do better'. Some mothers feel that the main role of the father is to enforce discipline and to punish ('Why should I always be the bad guy in the family?').

Children need to be loved by their parents. For babies that is almost enough (provided they are kept warm and clean and fed). For older children, it is necessary for their happiness and development that they do things with their family: sometimes play together, do household chores together, discuss things together. A single mother can supply love for both parents if necessary. She can do things with her children as they grow up. It isn't easy, but it's usually possible, and most single mothers do a very good job of it when their children are small.

When adolescence comes along, a boy needs more than love and being part of the family. He needs to identify with an adult male whom he admires, and who respects him. Ideally this would be his father. Before industrial development, it was common for a boy to follow his father in whatever work he did. Whether it was working on a farm, or at a trade, a boy would learn from his father from the age of about 14, from the beginning of adolescence. This is rather uncommon now, and a boy often knows very little of what his father does at work. Even if he follows his father's profession, it is likely that his training will be at school or university or with other people. So a father needs to make special arrangements to be with his son during the teenage years.

This is where problems arise in our modern society. A father may not be around. He may have married again and have other children by a new marriage. He may be so busy that he can't spare time for his son. He may be expending so much emotional energy on disciplining his son, that there isn't much time or energy left for just enjoying each other's company.

Even if a father and his son do have good times together, and clearly express their love for each other, a boy at this age needs to be admired and respected. He may be hopeless at sport, struggling at school or have health problems, but there must be something that a father could be proud of. Maybe art, woodwork, drama, fixing things, fishing, breeding budgerigars — something that a boy can do well and achieve. A boy needs to know that his father is boasting to other members of the family or to his friends about something the boy is good at.

A single mother who has spent many years looking after her children, in the absence of their father, may be a bit sad or resentful that her teenage son wants to start spending time with his father. She may feel, very understandably, that her son's father hasn't earned the right to enjoy the boy's friendship after leaving her with all the early childhood worries and responsibility.

This feeling can be just as true for a mother in an intact family, who has battled on without much support from her husband, whose interests may have been outside the home, or who may have had personal problems of his own.

Most mothers, however, will realize that a son needs his father for his adolescent development, and that it won't spoil the relationship she has built up with him over the critical childhood years. She has to let go a bit, and even encourage a renewed relationship between father and son. She may need to be careful not to run down the boy's father, nor relive the difficult times they may have had together.

Of course, some men weren't cut out to be fathers, or husbands for that matter. Alcohol or drug abuse or a violent nature may have made them poor role models for their children. In that case, a mother may need to find a person who can fill the role of father figure. She should know that that person cannot completely fulfil the role, and her boy might resent it if he tries too hard.

WHAT CAN A FATHER DO WITH HIS TEENAGE SON?

Fathers should try to make time to spend with their teenage sons. There must be some things that they can enjoy together.

I often ask boys who feel that their father is too busy to do things with them, or not interested, what they would like. The most common things are going camping together or fishing together. It is not enough for the whole family to go. It has to be something father and son do together. A weekend now and again is enough. Playing a game in the evening after the evening meal is good. Fathers shouldn't sulk if their sons beat them at sport, nor should they let them win. A bit of friendly competition between the men of the family is good.

What happened to Peter? His mother told me that he was fine. He was still living with his father, had got a job and was thinking of going back to part-time study. When he came over to visit his mother and sisters, he was much more amiable to be with, and there was no further trouble with the police.

Rules for unruly teenagers

Everyone needs rules in life if we are to live safely and peacefully with everyone else. Teenagers need rules too, even if they do break them sometimes. Some people say that you shouldn't give teenagers rules, because that will just give them something to break. Not so. If you ask teenagers whether there should be rules in their house, they will say that of course there should, so long as the rules are sensible and appropriate for their age group.

Actually rules give teenagers some security. It helps them to know how far they can go and what to expect if they go too far. They may break the rules. They may test them to the full. They may argue that the rules are unfair. They may say that none of their friends have to follow such stupid rules. They can and probably will say and do all that, but they still need rules. And they know they do.

Sometimes teenagers use rules to get out of doing something that they don't really think they should do, but which their friends are trying to persuade them to do. *'I can't, my parents won't let me.' 'I'd really like to, but I'm grounded.'* That way, their parents can take the blame.

TEENAGERS SHOULD HELP MAKE THE RULES

There should be some time set aside for both parents to sit down with their teenager to agree on rules. Now that their teenager is growing up, he or she can make sensible decisions about what is reasonable and what fits in with the rest of the family. The rules should be a bit flexible sometimes, but there

I WILL MAKE MY BED.... JUST AS SOON AS I .... FIND IT!

KEEP OUT

parents would like, but sometimes there has to be some give and take, so long as basic family standards are maintained.

Perhaps there are cultural differences of what children can and can't do. Parents still have the final say, but they might consider that by the time their children are into their mid-teens, they are living in two worlds: the world of their family, and the world of their friends. It isn't easy to live in a teenage world if your expected behaviour is very different to everyone else. It also isn't easy to live in two worlds with different sets of rules: your family's and those of everyone else.

WHAT SORT OF RULES SHOULD YOU SET?

You shouldn't have too many rules: it just makes everyone confused. On the other hand, if you don't have some rules, teenagers don't know what is expected of them. They might be upset when you are angry with them if they don't know what they are doing wrong.

It isn't possible to set out rules that would apply to every family. The age and degree of maturity will determine rules too. What is appropriate for a 13 year old would be inappropriate for a 15 year old, and even more so for an 18 year old.

Here are some areas about which it would be sensible to have discussions with your teenager, and then to decide about the rules that you set: bedtime, household chores, keeping his or her room clean, homework, parties, smoking and alcohol. After the rules have been discussed, your teenager can hardly be surprised when you are disappointed or angry if the rules are broken. Nor can they reasonably complain about penalties or punishment that you impose.

are standards that parents set, which are important to them, and which their children should try to stick to.

Every family has its own standards. It's part of the family culture. It may be different from other families, but within families there is a special link with each other that makes them unique.

On the other hand, parents will recognize that their son or daughter has to fit into what his or her friends do sometimes. This may not be really what the

BEDTIME

This is a source of irritation for many families with a teenager. Night-time is when many teenagers come alive. Going to bed is very boring. The homework may not be done. There is something very good on television, which mustn't be missed and which all their friends will be watching. Even if excuses run out, teenagers can take hours actually getting into bed, and then hours turning the light out and the radio off.

You will probably decide on one time for bed on school nights and one time for holidays and the weekend. The main point is to make sure that teenagers get enough sleep. (Sleep is discussed in Chapter 9.)

HOUSEHOLD CHORES

All children should make some contribution to the family's wellbeing by helping with household chores and jobs. Chores and jobs should be clearly understood. They should be valued. They should be appreciated. And they should be done.

KEEPING HIS OR HER ROOM CLEAN

All teenagers expect to do this, and it is good training for adult life. Mothers are not slaves. If a mother picks up her son's dirty clothes and rubbish, she is going to produce an adult who will be impossible to live with because he expects everyone to do things for him, especially his wife.

If a teenager's room looks a mess, that's their look out. Either shut the door so you can't see the mess or, better still, make your teenager clean it out on certain agreed days. Don't feel personally responsible for the mess if friends or neighbours drop by: you aren't responsible, and it's part of the teenager's training.

HOMEWORK

This is a high priority if your teenager wants to complete secondary schooling. Homework is really a contract between the school and the student, but it often happens that some supervision is needed, at least in the early teen years. Discuss with your teenager how much time they need for homework and when they feel it should be done. When they get home from school? After the evening meal? After their favourite TV show? Whatever the time, it shouldn't be last thing at night, when they are too tired to do it and it means staying up late.

Some teenagers need help in organizing their time and homework and assignment schedules. You may need to decide to what extent you are expected to help organize your teenager's schedules or to remind him or her to do it. You will probably need to help with some of the work in doing assignments and getting them done in time.

PARTIES

Parties are the thing that keeps some teenagers sane. Teenagers really look forward to parties, and when they get there, they can forget their worries and have fun. They are also likely to forget some of the rules you have set, unless you remind them and make it clear that you regard the rules as important. Alcohol and smoking — to say nothing of marijuana and sex — are important issues, and the extent to which you feel you should discuss them depends on your teenager, their level of maturity, and the degree to which you feel that you can trust them to make the right decisions.

The most important rules, at least in early and mid-teenage, are knowing where your teenager is, when you can expect them home, and how they are getting home. This is partly for your own peace of mind, but also to protect your teenager, and keep them safe.

(For more on parties, see Chapter 6.)

SMOKING

You probably don't want your teenager to smoke. Say so. If you yourself or other people in the family smoke, it may be hard to stop your teenager. After all, if it's good enough for you, why not for him or her? But you can still try, for the good of your teenager's health.

(For more on smoking, see Chapter 10.)

ALCOHOL

Many teenagers drink at parties. But not all. If any teenagers have cars, and are driving home after the party, they must not drink at all. Your teenager must not be driven home from a party by someone who has been drinking: this is when many tragedies happen. Whether your teenager drinks at the party depends on them, but you can certainly make it clear what you would like.

Teenagers who get drunk at parties often try hard to prevent their parents from finding out. Be alert. See your teenager when they get home. Vomiting after parties usually means a hangover (not food poisoning!).

(For more on alcohol, see Chapter 10.)

Discipline for difficult teenagers

A group of Year 11 students were discussing the question of discipline with me recently. It wasn't that they had a problem themselves, but they wanted to talk about some of their friends who had difficulty obeying rules at school. These friends were getting into a lot of trouble, and some had been suspended. The group felt the suspension was reasonable, but it was upsetting the class and worrying their friends.

'The trouble is that people can't make us do anything if we really don't want to,' one of them said. 'All they can do at school is give us a detention or, if it's very serious, they can suspend us.'

Someone else suggested that they should bring back corporal punishment. 'That would have some effect, and it would be all over quickly so we wouldn't resent it so much like we do detentions.'

'At home my parents can't do much if I muck around — they just ground me, but I can get out if I really want to.'

'Mine just send me to my room. Big deal — I'd rather be there anyway. I've got my own television and I get away from my really annoying family.'

DISCIPLINE ISN'T THE SAME AS PUNISHMENT

Ideally, discipline comes from within oneself, but in childhood it needs to be imposed. This leads to school rules, and teachers who make sure that they are obeyed. At home, parents make the rules. That is usually easy when children are young and eager to please their parents. Young children usually know quite well when they have been naughty, and are not too surprised when they are punished.

Parents know that their children's behaviour is developed by rewards when they are good (praise is reward enough most of the time), and punishment when they are bad (ranging from ignoring them to more severe punishments). The same is generally true for adolescents, but it doesn't always work so well, and sometimes they resent it. A sharp slap isn't so effective, and is liable to be labelled as child abuse; they might even hit back. 'Go to your room' might be seen as humiliating them; grounding them might be seen as an intrusion on their personal and social life.

Still, teenagers do need discipline, and they know this quite well. If it's fair (or seems so to them), they won't resent it, however much they will be angry with their parents and with themselves at the time.

TEENAGERS DEVELOP SELF-DISCIPLINE

Parents hope that their teenagers will eventually develop self-discipline. Self-discipline puts order in teenagers' lives and protects them from doing silly things. It enables them to focus on what they are doing, even if they would rather be doing something else. Any serious musician needs self-discipline to practise properly. Any serious sportsman or sportswoman needs self-discipline to train properly. Effective study for school exams and entry to tertiary education needs immense self-discipline for all but the brightest students.

For most teenagers, self-discipline may be a question of delaying some pleasure or putting off doing something that they really want to do. To be able to do this is a sign of developing maturity, of growing up. Self-discipline can be doing homework on time, or meeting a deadline for handing in an assignment. Self-discipline can also be not getting drunk at a party.

If a teenager doesn't seem to be developing self-discipline, they may need help. If that doesn't work, self-discipline needs to be imposed. If that doesn't work, they may need to be punished. The threat of punishment may be the one thing that they need to help them develop self-discipline.

HOW DO YOU HELP YOUR TEENAGER DEVELOP SELF-DISCIPLINE?

This is best started well before puberty. If children are used to their parents giving them firm and consistent guidelines for behaviour, then they become used to discipline. They expect it, and they find it easier to make their own self-discipline when they become adolescents.

On the other hand, if Daddy's little girl can twist his arm to give in to all of her demands, even when her mother has said no, this same girl, when she is older, will reject discipline and expect to have her immediate wishes gratified even when they are quite unreasonable. The same is just as true for boys.

If rules are kept consistently (but not rigidly), and if both parents are in agreement about them (or at least in agreement about how they are to be imposed), then most children and teenagers will find it easier to accept them. Of course house rules are for everyone, not just one child or one teenager.

LEARNING TO DEVELOP SELF-CONTROL

Teenagers can learn to develop self-control and discipline by receiving firm guidance from their parents, by planning ahead so they aren't carried away by impulses, and by suffering the consequences of their own actions.

It is not always helpful to bale out your teenagers every time they get into trouble. If your teenager breaks something, they should pay for it. If your teenager hasn't the money, they must earn it or borrow the money from you and pay it back. If your teenager breaks the law, it may be quite useful for the police to give them a bit of a scare. Protecting your teenager from all the consequences of their actions may just make them feel that they can get away with it.

BOTH PARENTS SHOULD BE CONSISTENT IN IMPOSING RULES

Most people have their own ideas about how to bring up children and how to treat teenagers. So it is not surprising that a mother and father will often differ in their individual approach to their teenager. Sometimes one parent thinks that the other is too harsh, while that parent may think that the other gives in too easily. This can so easily develop into an argument in front of the teenager, who is confused, tends to take sides, takes advantage of the disagreement and sees it as their chance to get away with whatever they want to do.

It is usually wise for parents to discuss their approach to discipline before they confront their teenager. Then they can present a united front. This prevents the teenager splitting the family up, putting one parent off side, and getting away with something that may not be in their best interests.

Better still, family rules can usually be discussed harmoniously by the whole family around the dinner table before a conflict arises at all. Rules are easier to keep if you yourself have taken part in making them. If there are wide age differences between the children in the family, then it might be better for parents to discuss rules with the teenager alone. It makes the teenager feel more responsible, and saves him or her from feeling put down in front of younger brothers or sisters.

A difficulty arises when a younger teenager thinks that an older sibling has unfair privileges. *'She can stay out late, why can't I? Don't you trust me like you trust her?' 'He doesn't have to do the washing up, why should I? I don't care if he is doing his final exams, it isn't fair.'*

Parents just have to adjudicate as best they can if their 13 year old is being illogical, but be sure that you listen to your young teenager if he or she has a good point to make. And consider whether you are really being fair. Should there really be different rules for boys and girls? Sure, girls are at greater risk than boys if they are on public transport at night, but this is a practical issue which should not be confused with family rules. Should a younger child get away with things just because they've always been the baby? Should a teenager never be trusted just because they have let you down in the past?

How can parents punish their teenagers if they do wrong?

Teenagers know they deserve punishment if they do wrong. They expect it, and they recognize that it helps them behave sensibly. The difficulty is knowing how and when to punish. There seem so few options. It may be helpful to discuss the question of punishments with your teenager. You will probably find that they have their own ideas on the subject, and they may be very reasonable and effective. The right time to discuss punishments is when everyone is in the right mood, not when there has been a fight or when you are actually about to administer punishment.

Of course, what would be an appropriate punishment for a young child may be quite inappropriate for a teenager. A 16 year old will expect to be treated differently from her 13-year-old sister. Even so, there still need to be consistent rules and consequences. That is what happens in modern society, and that is how parents can help their teenagers prepare for the real world.

SHOULD YOU GIVE WARNING ABOUT PUNISHMENT?

Usually yes. That is the advantage of having house rules that have been discussed in advance with the teenager: it gives an opportunity to discuss appropriate punishments. That way there is much less risk of resentment. The punishment may be well understood and agreed upon by parents and teenagers, and none the less effective for it. Probably easier to enforce, too. And it may save the mother or father who hands out the punishment from being regarded as the cruel and unreasonable ogre of the family (then everyone shares the blame for the punishment, including the teenager himself or herself).

CORPORAL PUNISHMENT IS OUT

Hitting a teenager is not acceptable to them, or to society, as it once was. Some people think this change is a triumph for human rights, while others argue that corporal punishment is a parent's natural response to a child doing something wrong or dangerous, and that it is is effective, immediate, quick, and soon over. After all, children hit each other. Some animals slap their young to teach them.

Whatever the argument, hitting a teenager is no longer an option. They would almost certainly resent it bitterly and might feel humiliated, and it could be regarded as abuse. It is so easy to go too far, especially when you are angry and your teenager is shouting insults at you.

DENYING PRIVILEGES

It can be very reasonable to stop a teenager doing something he or she likes, as a punishment. It might be stopping the watching of a TV show, especially a favourite soapie. It might be denying the use of Nintendo, computer games or the video.

It is important to agree on the time the punishment is in force. Having decided on the duration, don't relent because you have second thoughts (unless you feel that you really have been unjust), or because the soapie has reached a critical stage that can't possibly be missed. Your teenager can find out what happened from friends next day, when sharing views with them about his or her parents' terrible unfairness. Don't video-tape the program, either: that rather defeats the purpose of the punishment.

GROUNDING

This is probably the commonest form of punishment given to teenagers these days and, as their teenage friends probably get grounded too, it is usually acceptable to them as reasonable punishment. It usually hurts in the way it should as a punishment, as going out with friends is one of the most important and enjoyable activities a teenager has.

Make sure that you know what it is that you are preventing your teenager going to when you impose this punishment. Their misdeed may be so serious that all activities, including best friends' parties, should be banned. On the other hand, you may feel that although the grounding was well deserved, to miss some very important event, such as a rock concert that has been paid for and looked forward to for months, may be imposing too great a punishment.

FINES

It's very reasonable to impose fines, particularly if your teenager has done something that costs money to repair, like smashing his bedroom door. A fine is much better than denying pocket money or an allowance. Pocket money, once agreed upon, should not be dependent on good behaviour, or on doing household chores. Fines, on the other hand, are a common form of punishment that both hurts the teenager and helps recompense for misdeeds.

It is good training for the teenager to hand over a sum of money, rather than merely having it deducted from an allowance. This reinforces the fact that it was a punishment. It expiates the sin. It gives the teenager a sense of concluding the event: that it's all over and paid for. Reduced allowance, on the other hand, may cause resentment, even though the result (loss of the teenager's money) is the same.

If the teenager hadn't actually caused damage or some extra expense for the family, perhaps the fine could go to charity, or be placed 'in trust', to return to the teenager at a later date.

DOING HOUSEHOLD JOBS

This is a reasonable form of punishment, and has the advantage of making the punishment a positive contribution to the family rather than a negative imposition on the teenager. It is better if it is something extra and different from the usual household chores that everyone has to do. It might mean painting the back fence, or spring-cleaning the garage, or making a new dog kennel.

The disadvantage of this form of punishment is that doing jobs around the home should be part of every child's contribution to the family. It is much the same as a parent cooking the meals or paying the electricity bill. It is their way of helping everyone else, and should be valued as such.

If you feel that way, as I do, it may be better not to link household chores to punishment. Only the family can decide about this.

Thinking ahead and considering consequences

SOME TEENAGERS DO THINGS WITHOUT THINKING

Peter had got into trouble just once too often, and the police had called around to talk to him and his parents. His mother felt there was something wrong with Peter. It seemed to her that he had a real problem in the way he behaved, particularly as he didn't really seem to her to be a bad boy despite some of the things he had done.

'My son never seems to think about what he is doing. He is always getting into trouble. We have long talks about his behaviour, and he seems sorry and understands what he has done. Then next day he goes off with his mates and does something terrible all over again. Punishing him doesn't seem to make any difference.'

Peter's mother was describing a common problem for some teenagers. They don't seem to pause to consider the consequences of what they might do. They just go and do it. This may seem natural for younger children, but adolescents should have matured enough to think twice before doing something silly.

The difficulty for them seems to be that these teenagers have difficulty in thinking ahead and forming an idea of what follows any action. They may not mean harm to themselves or to others but it doesn't cross their mind what consequences there may be to what they do.

TEENAGERS LEARN TO REASON WITH THEMSELVES AND THINK AHEAD

'Maybe it would be fun to set fire to the bicycle shed at school. It would serve the principal right: he doesn't care about us kids. The fire would be excellent, and maybe the school would be closed for a few days.'

Something like this probably crosses the mind of many teenagers at times, particularly if they have had a bad time from one of the teachers. Then they get thinking:

'Some of the kids may have their bikes in the shed, and they would be damaged. It would be a fairly silly way of getting back at the school, and it probably wouldn't cause much grief to the teachers anyway. And there is a good chance we would get caught, which would mean the police coming round, and Mum and Dad getting upset. And we might have to pay for the damage. So we won't do it after all.'

It seemed that Peter couldn't think ahead and reason it out like this very easily. If he had, he wouldn't have got into the trouble he was in. He needed help in thinking ahead, of allowing his mind to consider any impulsive plan before carrying it out.

If a teenager hasn't reached the stage when their thinking can do this, they may need to rely on the threat of punishment to delay impulsive actions. Parents can warn and discuss and reason with their teenager, but it is often interpreted as nagging, and quickly forgotten.

Testing rules

TEENAGERS LIKE TO TEST OUT RULES

Teenagers like to test how far they can go with rules. What they can get away with. It is not that they are openly rebellious (though they might be), so much as they are challenging adult views that they feel are being imposed on them.

Another difficulty for them is that they tend to live in the present. If they are having a good time with their friends, they are liable to forget rules they had agreed to earlier.

IF REASONING FAILS, YOU ARE BOSS

Finally. You have had your reasonable discussion. Everyone has had their say. Your teenager doesn't agree, and makes unreasonable or unacceptable demands.

Then you may have to remind your teenager that home is not a democracy. It's your house. You pay the bills. You are responsible for his or her health and safety. You are boss. Your teenager doesn't agree? Tough.

Things that annoy teenagers, and keeping peace in the family

Some teenagers seem to get angry very easily, especially with their parents and brothers and sisters. Little things really set them off: advice or requests that seem perfectly reasonable to parents; a sibling's teasing that seems pretty harmless (probably no more harmful than the teenager has given at times); chance remarks about behaviour or hairstyle or homework.

To make matters more irritating, the teenager seems able to take the same remarks from others — friends or other adults — without getting annoyed at all.

Parents have every right and responsibility to advise, make comments to and request things from their teenagers, and even make demands. Sometimes however, the timing is wrong. It is not the best time to comment adversely on clothes or hairstyle just when the teenager is off to meet friends. It is usually a disaster to bring up the matter of the untidy bedroom and the dirty laundry when you are already in the middle of a argument about homework.

The trouble is that these are the very times that, as a parent, you are thoroughly fed up and feel inclined to make remarks that infuriate. You are already cross with your teenage son because he's had a bad school report, so you tell him about his essential slovenliness, laziness and lack of consideration for others in the household. 'Motivation' and 'attitude' are good words to start a fight. No wonder that your teenager feels like punching a hole in the bedroom wall — anyway, it's better than swinging a punch at you.

You comment on your teenage daughter's strange make-up and awful hairstyle when she has spent hours getting it right to go out with friends. She probably has doubts herself, but she'll be better off yelling at you and storming out the door than bursting into tears (and wrecking her make-up and being miserable with her lost confidence).

Even if the time is right — your teenager in a good mood and is hanging around and seems receptive to reasonable discussion — there are some things you probably can't bring up without a fight on your hands. If they are important, so be it, and be prepared to put up with comments such as *'You're stupid'*, *'You can't make me and I won't'*, *'I wish I could leave home'*, *'It's so unfair'*, even *'You don't love me and you never have'*. Most teenagers know very well how to really upset their parents if they put their mind to it. Don't necessarily assume that they really mean what they say in these circumstances.

WHAT ARE SOME OF THE THINGS THAT MOST ANNOY TEENAGERS?

- Not being allowed to dress the way they want to. *'You can't make me.'* You may not like what they choose to wear, but they do, and that's important (to them).

- Adverse comments on hairstyle. *'You're out of date, and anyway, what's it got to do with you?'* Hair has always been very important at all ages.

- Strict house rules if they are imposed on some of the family and not on others. 'Unreasonable, unfair and stupid.'

- Being told to do house chores if they have never been expected to do them before, or if the others don't have to do anything. 'Not fair — why can't she do it?' If children haven't had to help around the house when they were young, they will probably resent it when they are given chores as a teenager. It's always best to start young.

- Imposing curfews that appear to be very different to those of their friends. 'So unfair.' The same discussion is probably going on at his or her friend's house.

- Being told that they are fat, thin, short, tall. They know this already.

- Adverse comments on their friends. Having a friend and belonging to a group — any friend or any group — may be so very important that it overrides any consideration of suitability or parental approval.

- Being accused of not doing homework. The justice of the accusation has no bearing on the matter.

HOW DO YOU COPE WITH THESE FIGHTS AND ARGUMENTS?

There are some arguments that you can never win, because teenagers feel very strongly about some things, and to give in would be even more painful than the fight itself. Some adults are like this too. Sometimes I ask families: 'Where did the teenager get their stubborn nature from?' Often mother or father own up (or are exposed by the rest of the family as the villain who passed on the bad-temper genes).

There are some things that you can try, however.

1. Don't waste emotional energy by picking an argument that you can't win

Teenagers can be just as stubborn as their parents, and can be quite powerful in an argument. There are some things that you may have to agree to disagree on. Perhaps your teenager will come around to your viewpoint when they are a little older.

2. If something is really important for your teenager's safety or health, and you can't get through to him or her, involve a third party

Choose someone who is acceptable to you both, to help your teenager see your viewpoint. Perhaps the family doctor, a school counsellor, or a respected relative. Teenagers can sometimes be more reasonable with people who aren't emotionally involved and who don't seem to be taking sides. If all fails, safety and health must take precedence. Make the rules and be firm about them.

3. Try to avoid arguments about trivial or unimportant things

It's astonishing how bitter and violent arguments can become about silly things that may not matter so much in themselves, but become a major issue because of the hurtful things that are said, or because neither the child nor the parent are prepared to admit that he or she might have been wrong.

4. Try to discuss important issues when you are both in the right mood

There may never be a completely right time to confront your teenager about contentious matters like going out at night or suitability of friends or a bad school report or your attitude towards smoking. But there certainly are bad times, such as when you are both tired or stressed out or in a hurry or just five minutes before a favourite soap is due on TV.

5. Try to listen to your teenager's viewpoint

This can be very boring and can take a long time because teenagers don't always find it easy to express themselves. Most teenagers are more likely to listen to you if they think you are listening to them. You may have to let them give their viewpoint first before they get too angry to discuss it at all.

Privacy: who needs it?

'And another thing, I think that you go through my rubbish.' Shane was sounding off to his mother during a meeting he and I had arranged, to clear up some of the difficulties that he had with his family.

His mother was surprised to hear a lot of the things he told her, but she couldn't understand that there was anything special about rubbish. 'Naturally I see it when I tidy up. And I don't like what I see sometimes.'

'Yeah, exactly, you shouldn't go

6. Make sure both parents express similar views. It is best if both are present at any important discussion

Arguments on important matters that affect the way the family functions are best resolved with all the family present. Teenagers are fairly good at dividing the family up if they can get away with it. Beware: it's not in their best interests if they succeed. Parents may find it helpful to have a prior discussion together to resolve any differences and to plan strategies.

7. Share humour

Joke with your teenager. But don't laugh at your teenager: it only puts him or her down. Your teenager may not think it's all that funny to laugh at his or her new pimple or disastrous attempt at a new hair colour.

8. Be prepared to apologize if you think you may have been wrong (and even sometimes if you don't)

It isn't easy, especially if you think that it is your teenager who really owes you an apology, but it can make him or her feel a bit better about a grievance. (But don't expect your teenager to accept your apology graciously.)

9. Give credit to the good things that your teenager does when you are listing all his or her faults

Sometimes teenagers are deeply hurt when they have been trying to improve and all they hear are their bad points.

looking at my stuff.'
'But your rubbish?
I have to throw it out,
you know.'
'Well, it's my rubbish.'

TEENAGERS NEED THEIR PRIVACY

Parents don't always realize how important privacy is to teenagers. Or what things they regard as private and personal. Almost all their personal things are at home (there's nowhere else for them, even their school locker isn't always safe), so they have to trust their family to leave their stuff alone.

Shane wasn't talking about *rubbish* (though perhaps there were things in it that he wanted to keep private) but his *privacy* — his own right to keep things to himself if he wanted to. And a person's cast-off rubbish tells you quite a lot about that person.

It's hard for parents, mothers particularly, to think of a teenager's bedroom as a private place. They are so used to tidying up, putting clothes away, stacking toys and cleaning under the bed when their child was small. If they didn't, their child's room would be a horrible mess. When their child becomes an adolescent however, mothers are expected to stop all this and leave their child's room alone, treating it as their child's private domain. But do teenagers clean their room to their mother's standards?

AHH… I'M JUST TIDYING UP!

Maybe once a month, and then only after a massive row. Many girls are extremely good at keeping their room clean and neat, but boys are usually terrible. So what do most mothers do? They go in occasionally to check on the mess and take smelly clothes off to be washed and replace them with clean ones. These things probably have to be done, but that's when they are in danger of invading their teenager's privacy.

It's understandable that teenagers feel that way of course. Parents also need their own privacy, and usually don't like their teenagers fossicking amongst their possessions, particularly in their bedroom. By the time a child has entered teenage, he or she feels the same way: a need to have some times and places that are essentially their own, and where even their parents shouldn't enter without being invited. It's part of developing a sense of one's own identity, and not just being part of the family.

SHOULD PARENTS ALWAYS KNOW WHAT THEIR TEENAGER IS UP TO?

Another point: teenagers might have things that you wouldn't like them to have (they often do). Maybe these things are fairly harmless (but objectionable), such as certain magazines, or not so harmless, such as cigarettes. Or a 15-year-old girl might have decided that it would be safer for her to go on the pill, but couldn't face upsetting her mother about it. If this girl were your daughter, how would you and she feel if you found the packet of pills hidden in one of her drawers?

Is it better that you don't know about some of these things? Or do you feel that it is important to you to know exactly what your teenager is up to, for his or her own sake and for your peace of mind? There is something else to take into account: it may be that you pay a heavy price for seeking to know all about your teenager, as you may be betraying your teenager's trust in you to respect his or her privacy. It's a real dilemma for some parents, and there is no right answer except

to talk it over with your teenager.

Families need to discuss with their teenager what arrangements they can agree to for caring for his or her room, clothes and private possessions. Sometimes a teenager has to share a room with a brother or sister, and it is always helpful to have some rules about respecting each other's personal things, however well they get on with each other. Above all, parents must realize that most teenagers like to have a place where they can be alone when they want to be.

TEENAGERS ALSO HAVE PRIVATE THOUGHTS AND WORRIES

A very distressed mother brought her daughter's diary to show me one day. She had found it in Sara's undies drawer when she went to her room to put away her clean clothes. 'I didn't know whether to read it or not,' she said. 'On the one hand, she must have known I'd find it when I put her clothes away, and she did leave it on top. On the other hand, diaries are rather private.'

Anyway, she had read it, and received a bad shock. Sara had written a despairing entry about losing her friends, about life not being worth living and about leaving home and school.

I suggested that Sara had probably wanted her mother to know how unhappy she was but didn't know how else to tell her. Whether she should or should not have read the diary, she could hardly ignore an entry that expressed such misery.

Privacy extends well beyond a teenager's room and what he or she keeps in it of course. Teenagers will have private thoughts they may not want to share with their parents. Sometimes, however, these worries may seem overwhelming, and they may not feel able to tell their parents about them. They may use different ways to let them know: hints in their conversation, bad moods, and in Sara's case, her diary.

Sometimes teenagers may seek counselling if they have personal problems. They may not want their parents to know what things are discussed, or even what their problems are. To insist on sharing these private things may also be intruding on their privacy. It will probably make parents sad that their teenager doesn't want to share everything with them, especially the things that really worry their teenager, but it is often a sign of the teenager's developing maturity,

and in that sense is good. It may also mean that the teenager doesn't want to add to their parents' worries by sharing their own. Sooner or later, however, the teenager may feel ready to share these problems with their family, and that will be the time when the family's help will be most appreciated and most effective.

Sara's mother did tell her that she had seen her diary, and she understood how unhappy she must feel. Sara expressed fury that her mother had read her very private diary, but a little later agreed that she could do with some help, and agreed to see the school counsellor.

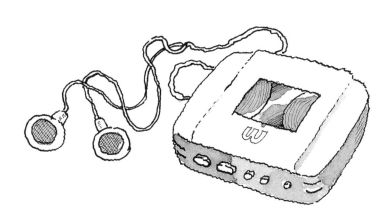

CHAPTER 4

DEPRESSION, SUICIDE AND ANGER

Depression

Fifteen-year-old Stephen came to see me because he had dropped out of school, despite a very good previous school record. It was not at all clear why he just dropped school, but there were other things that worried his parents. He wasn't looking after himself very well. He seldom showered, he slept in late, he had got drunk on several occasions and once had got into a fight which led to police becoming involved.

Alone, Stephen made it very clear that he was depressed. He was often sad and miserable. He saw no hope for his future. There was no point in going to school, as there was little likelihood that he would still be alive when he was 20. There wasn't a lot of point in getting up in the mornings, and anyway he was usually hungover. Alcohol was just about the only thing that made him reasonably happy. That and friends whom his parents disapproved of because they had also dropped out of school and drank heavily.

Depression used to be thought of as an adult disorder. We now know that many teenagers feel depressed at times. This can be severe, and may be linked to the rising rates of suicide amongst teenagers in our community.

A large survey amongst secondary school students in Victoria showed that about 7% of boys and girls in Year 7 (their first year of secondary school) were mildly or moderately depressed at the time of the survey. The rate rose markedly for both boys and girls, but much more so for girls. By Year 11, 25% of girls showed the signs of either mild or moderate depression. The rate for boys was 14%. These alarming findings are consistent with other surveys of teenagers both in Australia and in North America.

The signs of depression in adolescents are usually different from those in adults, and the treatment is certainly different, as anti-depressant drugs are usually rather unhelpful in treatment.

Teenagers who become severely depressed fail to cope with the pressures in their life. They tend to do poorly at school, or to drop out. They stop playing sport and lose interest in pursuits and hobbies that they had previously enjoyed. Life seems boring and futile with no future. They have difficulty in concentrating, and feel apathetic and lazy. They may feel unattractive and unlovable. If they break a close relationship, as they probably will, this reinforces their feelings. They tend to feel hopeless and helpless. They may start to think of harming themselves and ending their life.

Sometimes they will get headaches and other symptoms. They may have difficulty in getting to sleep, and then in getting up in the morning. Some will meet up with other teenagers who are also not coping well with their lives, and may use drugs, take risks, and become anti-social with acts of vandalism and theft. Others may become withdrawn and see little of their friends, spending their time in their room at home.

What can be confusing is that their behaviour may be so bad that no-one realizes that they are really depressed. They need active help with their depression, rather than punishment. It can also happen that the signs of depression may be confused with a physical illness.

The hopeful aspect of this gloomy picture is that teenagers can be helped to overcome depression. They do get better. It is important that depression be considered as a possible cause of unexplained bad behaviour, dropping out of school, and using drugs.

When Stephen's diagnosis of depression was made, his parents' attitude changed from anger to support. The police dropped charges and he was happy to see a psychiatrist. Stephen benefited from a number of meetings with his psychiatrist. He clarified some of the things that had led to his depression, and what had kept it going. He learnt how to overcome it without the use of drugs. He didn't get back to school, but he did get a job. He drank far less alcohol and found a very understanding and loving girlfriend.

Suicide, and hurting oneself

Megan was rushed by ambulance to a local hospital. She had been found by her older brother in her room. She was in coma and couldn't be roused. There was a note to her friends and parents on her desk. Fortunately she responded to treatment and next day told how she had taken 15 of her mother's sleeping pills, some Panadol tablets and almost half a bottle of whisky. She had wanted to die, but now she had survived, she felt embarrassed about it and didn't want to talk about it. She refused to see a psychiatrist, and said she wasn't going to repeat the attempt.

She did talk about it later, after she had gone home. She had been under a good deal of stress with a chronic illness. She wasn't doing well at school in her critical Year 10, and her parents' high expectations of her looked as if they would not be met. The reason for not coping so well recently was a very serious relationship with a boy. What seemed to have precipitated the suicide attempt was the boy telling her in a letter that they wouldn't see each other for a while, as he was moving interstate.

Suicide rates amongst male teenagers have increased over the last 10 years and suicidal gestures and self-harm have become common amongst teenagers of both sex, especially girls. It is not clear why this is so, although it does relate to the high rate of depression amongst teenagers. It is probably linked to the increased pressures at school, with the greater incidence of family breakdown, and with high parental expectations for their teenager at a time when there is a lot of competition for university places and jobs.

The possibility of suicide is often on parents' minds, particularly as so much is written about it in the papers, and shown on television. What leads to an adolescent trying to take his or her own life? Do teenagers really mean to kill themselves, or are they asking for help through a desperate gesture of despair? What do teenagers understand by death? Do they really mean to leave their friends and family for ever?

TEENAGERS WHO HURT THEMSELVES AND ENDANGER THEIR LIVES

For every suicide attempt that results in death, there may be as many as 500 that do not. Some, if not most, of these were not serious attempts to end life, but to hurt themselves, with the possibility of death: they just didn't care at the time. Girls are more likely to do this than boys, and do things like taking pills or poisonous substances, or cutting their wrists. Boys often use more violent means from which they cannot be rescued, like shooting or hanging themselves.

Teenagers who hurt themselves in this way often do so during a period of stress, when some event precipitates a crisis. It may be a broken relationship, a serious row with parents, or difficulty at school. They may have shared some of their worries with friends, but often they haven't. They may have told their mother they wanted to talk about something, but it was an awkward time when she was busy, and she put them off. Perhaps they interpreted this as lack of interest in their problem.

SOME SUICIDE ATTEMPTS SEEM TO BE QUITE IMPULSIVE

I remember a youth who had been caught breaking into a house with a group of older friends. He escaped from the police, only to hang himself in shame and misery at what his family would think. Fortunately one of his friends found him and cut him down in time to save his life. He was unconscious but survived. When I saw him later as he was recovering, he was still very upset, but relieved that his family was in fact standing behind him, and the police weren't going to proceed further. His hanging, which took him so close to death, had been an impulsive gesture.

Of course, even impulsive gestures like this usually have a background of emotional or relationship difficulties. Parents can't solve all their teenager's personal problems for them, and often they don't get told about them anyway. This boy's parents had been worried that he had been involved with the wrong crowd for some time, but they couldn't do anything about it.

WHAT CAN PARENTS DO TO PROTECT THEIR TEENAGER FROM SUICIDE?

They can help by being available when their teenager seems to want to talk about something. If the teenager seems distressed, parents can respond by being prepared to listen, by just recognizing that sometimes things can be overwhelming. If they can't help, they can take their teenager to someone outside the family. Teenagers don't like to worry their parents with their personal problems, but may be quite prepared to discuss it with someone else. Just be sure it is someone who is competent to help: a school counsellor, a family doctor or priest or psychologist. Your family doctor may recommend a specialist paediatric psychiatrist or adolescent physician.

ARE THERE ANY WARNING SIGNALS TO LOOK OUT FOR?

There are. Most of them may mean something else, or mean nothing at all important. All teenagers go through bad patches in their lives at times. However, parents should be on the lookout if their teenager seems to be unhappy or under stress.

- They may become isolated and withdrawn. They may be uncommunicative and spend most of their time alone.
- They may start giving away their most precious possessions to their brothers or sisters or special friends.
- They may become unusually affectionate after a period of being rather remote, as if they are saying goodbye.
- They may make a will.
- They may seem to be preoccupied with death.
- They may be thinking a lot about a loved relative or close friend who has died. Their thinking may include wanting to join them.
- They may want to seek advice from their doctor or counsellor, but not be able to say exactly what is on their mind. It is as if they are asking for help, but can't bring themselves to say what kind of help they need. A large proportion of teenagers who suicide have been to see their doctor within a few days before they took their lives.
- They may be showing signs of depression (see pages 50-51).
- They may be in despair about school work, and either work frantically or drop out when they could have been doing quite well.
- They may hint that they are letting you down. That they can't meet your expectations to succeed at school. That they are no good.

While these warning signs could at times apply to many teenagers, they should not be disregarded, especially if several of the signs are present.

One more thing: don't take a threat of suicide lightly. You may think that your teenager is just trying to frighten you during a row. They probably are, but you should take it seriously. Your teenager may mean it, and may be very disturbed if you just laugh it off.

Anger outbursts

Wayne had finally been suspended from school indefinitely, until something could be done about his violent temper. He was usually alright in class, but if someone annoyed him, he was uncontrollably aggressive. He had pushed a teacher against a window, breaking it. He had injured several students in violent outbursts. One parent was threatening to sue him and the school if he was allowed to return.

Other students didn't know how to handle him. He had been popular enough, and was good at sport, but now no-one liked to get too close to him. At home he had punched a hole through his bedroom wall and damaged the door in fits of rage.

You only have to look at a baby, furiously red in the face and yelling, with fists clenched and eyes screwed up, to know that anger is our earliest and often strongest emotion. When we feel sad, we can cry; when we feel happy, we can laugh and smile. But when we feel angry, we often take it out on people or things around us — either that or bottle it up and suffer feelings of blame and guilt.

Teenagers feel that way too. They may not have worked out satisfactory ways of dealing with life's day-to-day irritations. They may feel threatened by teachers or other students. They may have brought their frustrations from home, only to take them out on students who don't have the same power over them as their family. Unlike babies and toddlers, they are big and strong and can cause injury and damage.

Anger usually arises when a teenager feels threatened. Threats may come from a parent, a sibling, a fellow student, a teacher or even some innocent passer-by who gives them a funny look. Sometimes the anger comes from frustration when they can't do something that they feel they should be able to do. Sometimes their fury erupts when they expect something to happen, but it doesn't. Anger may arise very quickly. Without thought of the consequences, or caring anyway, they release their anger on someone or something.

IS IT JUST THEIR PERSONALITY, OR CAN SOMETHING BE DONE ABOUT IT?

Personality certainly plays a part. If you ask the family 'Where does he get his temper from?', they can almost always think of someone with a similarly short temper.

Some teenagers are easy going, and nothing seems to get them too angry. Some teenagers seem to react to threats by getting upset and feeling bad inside. They may feel guilty about their own feelings and inadequacies, or blame it on someone or something else, which doesn't usually resolve the problem. Other teenagers get pretty angry, even with trivial things, and show it.

In one sense, anger may be a healthy reaction to things that threaten the teenager. So long as it doesn't go too far, or hurt someone.

You normally can't change a teenager's personality, and you probably wouldn't want to. You may be able to help them come to terms with it, however, and learn to handle the drawbacks of a naturally quick temper.

WHAT CAN BE DONE TO REDUCE EXCESSIVE ANGER?

There are anger-control programs that have been devised to help teenagers. There may be one near where you live, and it could be worth finding out about this. A teenager would have to *want* to try out the program. The most effective programs are for groups of young people of similar age: the teenagers help each other, and they understand how the other people in the group feel.

On an individual basis, some child psychiatrists and psychologists have therapies that help. They may aim to modify a teenager's response to things that bring on excessive anger. They can also help a family work out ways of handling anger at home, and in giving help to their teenager.

IS THERE ANYTHING THAT PARENTS CAN DO?

Yes. First by understanding what the anger is all about.

Anger often arises from personal insecurity. Parents can help teenagers feel better about themselves, by identifying ways of boosting self-esteem, and by making sure that learning difficulties at school are recognized. Teenagers may need help with their frustrations at their poor performance at sport or in school. They may need assurance about their place in the family, and the esteem in which they are held by their parents.

If the teenager is prepared to sit down and talk about it with one or other parent (or better still, both), there are ways of helping:

- Help the teenager be aware that anger comes from within oneself, and it is not helpful to blame other people who may precipitate it. If the teenager can acknowledge that the anger is his own, and it is his own reaction to things around him, it may give him the first step to having the power to overcome it.

- Work out the degree of anger felt each time there has been an incident or outburst. There will be times when the anger has been mild and controlled; other times when there has been a violent outburst. Measuring the degree of anger helps to work out what strategies work in controlling anger. Use a scale of 10 possible points, where 10 is uncontrollable fury, and 1 is mild irritation. The teenager may judge that the time she smashed her tennis racquet, her anger was 9 out of 10. Measuring things often helps to control them, and gives us a means of assessing improvement. Teenagers usually quite like measuring things this way.

- Work out what it is that particularly angers him. It could be some threat to him that actually frightens him, and which leads to impulsive angry defence. Perhaps identifying the threat will diminish its power to frighten or anger. Perhaps it will lead to better strategies to handle it.

- Talk with her about the threats that cause anger. Sharing upsetting things with someone else can help, and lessen their power to make one angry.

- Get him to try to talk himself through his response to things that make him angry. This will sometimes make it unnecessary to lash out. If he can talk himself through it, he may not need to smash the door.

- Work on this thought with her: 'Consider forgiving the person who is making you angry. That person may have started it, and may be giving you a bad time, and it may be that person's own fault that you defend yourself. All this may be true, but if you can forgive your tormentor, it will actually increase your personal strength. It may even make things easier between the two of you. Once you have forgiven someone, you find that your anger goes.'

What happened to Wayne? He really needed this crisis before he could face up to the fact that he had a problem, and the problem was his own, not those who annoyed him.

He agreed to try an anger-control program with a group of boys with similar difficulties. I was a bit fearful for the person running the course: all those boys had the power to destroy each other. In fact, they mostly became good friends within the group.

Wayne enrolled in another school, made a new set of friends, and mended the hole in his bedroom wall with the help of his father. He called by to tell me he didn't need to see me any more.

CHAPTER 5

SCHOOL

Teasing: on getting a hard time at school

A teenager was discussing with me the problem of teasing at his school. He said that some boys seemed to get teased a lot, while others hardly ever. It wasn't just the smaller boys, or those who weren't good at sport, although they did seem to have a worse time of it. Anyone who was different seemed particularly liable to suffer from groups of other boys.

This boy had tried to work out how different boys handled teasing. He found that those who were teased a lot became very upset about it. They behaved in various ways. Some cried. Some tried to laugh it off. Some just walked away, trying to ignore it. Some tried to buy loyal supporters by giving them things. Some got mad and attacked their tormentors. Some felt it so badly that they often couldn't face school, and seemed to get sick quite often.

None of these responses seemed to work. If they cried the teasing got worse and more cruel. If they laughed at themselves, they lost any respect that they had for themselves and from others. Walking away sometimes worked, as the teasers did get bored with it, but it didn't earn the victims many friends. Who'd want to be friends with someone who couldn't handle teasing? Giving the teasers sweets or money shut them up for a few moments, and they took what was given, but it only increased the teasing in the long run. And it gave the victims a reputation for weakness, for trying to buy friends. Having a fight worked for some, but it was remarkable how often it was the victim of the teasing that got into trouble, not the people doing the teasing.

It almost seemed that whatever the unfortunate victim did was wrong. If a parent complained to the school it sometimes had a temporary effect, when a teacher might talk to some of the ringleaders, but it seldom solved the problem.

What made it worse was that no-one wanted to be associated with a kid who was always getting teased, in case it rubbed off on them. So they tended to get lonely and without friends. They often spent their lunch break in the library, and school became a very unhappy and lonely place for them.

WHAT CAN PARENTS DO IF THEIR TEENAGER IS GETTING TEASED?

Discuss it with your teenager. They might not want you to do anything, and would rather sort it out themselves. However, if they would like (or really need) help, parents might:

- Work out why your teenager is being teased. Is it because he or she is different? Too short, too fat, late puberty? It might be possible to do something about this. Perhaps it would be worth a visit to your doctor.

- Work on boosting your teenager's self-esteem. He or she could consider martial arts, going to a gym, playing drums (in the garage). A part-time job. Something that other teenagers can respect.

- Discuss with your teenager the possibility of him or her developing a new set of friendships outside the school or street environment where the teasing is occurring. Consider joining scouts, a youth group, a sport club.

- Discuss the problem with the school welfare coordinator or your teenager's year coordinator. There may be a school

TECHNIQUES TO AVOID BEING TEASED

Most teenagers get a bad time from other teenagers sometimes, and few escape the occasional taunt. So what do the teenagers who don't suffer from teasing do to avoid it?

There seem to be several techniques that they use. They probably do it almost automatically, but some teenagers have to learn how to respond to difficult situations when they are in a crowd of highly competitive and quarrelsome teenagers who get quite a bit of fun from others' discomfort.

1. Agree with the taunt, and follow with a light-hearted remark

'Hey Bulko, you're fat!'

'Yeah, I know. I went to get new jeans last week. None of them fitted me.'

It's pretty hard to make a big thing of this, and if the teenager doesn't get upset or angry, there isn't much point in going on with it.

2. Change the subject to distract the teaser

'...'

'Yeah. Hey, Steve, did you see that show on Channel 7 last night? What did you think of the great car chase?'

3. Explain your feelings to one or two friends (preferably big friends)

They can support you, and teasing won't seem so important.

'...'

'Get off his back, Jones, you're not so hot yourself.'

4. Get involved in a school activity

Choose an activity that keeps you busy, gets you some new friends and makes you less of a target for teasing. It's often the kid who hangs around without friends, and who has nothing to do, who gets a bad time. Maybe you can get into drama, work on the school play, join a chess club or computer group.

counsellor who could help with strategies to overcome the problem. There may be one or two ringleaders who could be moved to another class. Some schools have peer-support programs, and these can be very helpful in overcoming teasing and bullying.

- Make sure everything is alright for your teenager at home. He or she may need a lot of comfort and support at home if things are bad at school. Teenagers need a place where they can let their defences down and not have to defend themselves all the time. Encourage your teenager to talk about any difficulties they are having in peer relationships. If he's a boy, get his father involved in doing things with him.

- If teasing is a big problem, consider professional counselling. There are several techniques used by some psychologists and psychiatrists and youth workers that develop strengths in a teenager and put teasing into perspective.

School learning difficulties

Robert was causing a lot of concern to his parents since he started high school. He seemed to cope alright in primary school, except that he never enjoyed reading and his teachers always remarked on his untidy work, poor spelling and mistakes in handwriting.

Since he started secondary school, things had got worse. He seemed quite bright in classwork, took part in discussions, and enjoyed sport and art. But when it came to written work, he seemed to be falling further and further behind. To make matters worse, he wasn't handing in homework assignments. He always told his parents that there wasn't any homework, or that he had left it at school, or even that he had finished it in his lunch break. He got found out at parent–teacher interview, when his parents were most surprised to learn that he was so far behind. Robert said he hated reading, it took him hours to write an assignment and, when he did do it, it always got criticized and given a bad grade.

Despite detentions at school and supervision by his parents at home, things didn't improve much. All that happened was that he became angry and behaved badly at school. Reports started to mention that he 'should try harder', 'could do better', 'needs to be more careful with written work'.

Robert was eventually referred for physical and educational tests to try to find out why a boy who seemed otherwise bright was having so much trouble.

What these tests showed was that Robert was indeed of average intelligence but that he had definite difficulties in the way he was able to learn, especially in being able to translate his thoughts into written words. His mind had genuine trouble in remembering how letters looked on paper, how words were spelt. He had to spend so much time in puzzling things out that he couldn't finish work that other children could do in half the time. This had got him so frustrated that he felt like giving up trying. It was no wonder that he had started to muck around in class.

Many children have difficulties in learning at school, and this may be missed in primary school, only coming to everyone's attention when they are teenagers in secondary school. At this time much more may be expected of students, so teachers notice those who are having difficulties. Sometimes teenagers who have problems in learning get so frustrated by their difficulties, and by the need to put so much more effort into their work than other students, that they stop trying. Then they are blamed for this and their bad behaviour, without anyone quite knowing what has caused it.

This problem may affect about one in every ten students to some extent. One in a hundred has specific learning disabilities (like Robert) that need expert assessment to sort out why that student is having so much trouble.

Oddly enough, these problems seem to affect boys far more often than girls. We don't know why, but it's not usually a matter of intelligence.

Of course, if a student has an intellectual disability, he or she will have trouble learning at school, but this is often recognized in primary school or before. This is because such children tend to have trouble in all aspects of their work and may have been a worry for parents in early life before school started.

Assessment of school learning difficulties may be carried out by a teacher who is specially trained in educational assessment, or by a child psychologist who specializes in educational psychology. A paediatrician who has a special interest in school difficulties (and most do) may also be able to help sort out these problems and can look into other things like ill-health or visual and hearing difficulties. Sometimes medication for chronic illness may interfere with learning. Sometimes emotional problems, including difficulties at home, may stop teenagers studying to their capacity. Often learning difficulties run in families. Sometimes parents (and teachers, too) expect more from teenagers than is fair: after all, not everyone is academically inclined or needs to go to university. All these things can be sorted out by the educational psychologist or paediatrician working in consultation with the school.

After the learning difficulties have been assessed, it will be easier to work out strategies to help your teenager. These may be through the school program, with teachers taking into account the student's problems, or providing extra help. Sometimes remedial teaching may be recommended, and sometimes parents can give extra help. Sometimes working with a computer can make an enormous difference.

It usually turns out that it is not the student's fault at all that he is having school difficulties, and it helps him and his parents to know this. It is usual for a teenager to have some strengths in how he learns as well as some weaknesses. Knowing this, it can be helpful to build on those strengths, rather than emphasize the weaknesses. This may also help with self-confidence, which is so important in achieving well at school.

What happened to Robert? He was relieved to find a reason for his difficulties and to know that something could be done to overcome them. He found out that quite a lot of students who had the same specific learning difficulty (which used to be called 'dyslexia') had gone on to do very well at university and had successful professional careers.

There were a number of things that his school could do to help him overcome his difficulty. He was allowed to drop a foreign-language subject for instance, and in the spare period he was given extra help. He was allowed to use a computer for his assignments and his parents got a Spellcheck program to help correct his spelling (and incidentally help him to recognize his mistakes).

None of these things fixed his problems overnight, but Robert was much happier, worked better and started getting encouraging reports from his teachers, who got to understand him better.

Attention Deficit Disorder (ADD)

Alan was referred to me by his school. He had been to two other secondary schools (both of whom had found it impossible to teach him and were glad to see him leave). At this school, and at the age of 15, he was facing suspension once again. The problem seemed to be that he couldn't apply himself to learning in the classroom. He had never been able to sit still, and at primary school used to roam around the room, annoying other children.

He had had psychological and educational tests in primary school, and his parents were told that he was quite capable but needed more supervision at home if he was to reach his full potential. School reports said 'Could do better', 'Should learn to apply himself', 'Distracts other students', 'Doesn't finish tasks', 'Doesn't concentrate on what he is doing'.

Now that he was a teenager it was increasingly hard to supervise him and he often wagged school. When he was at school he seemed unable to concentrate for more that a few minutes, he was easily distracted by anything going on in or outside the
classroom, *and was distracting the other students. They seemed to be getting fed up with him (as was everyone else), and what friends he had were those who tended to get into trouble too.*

Alan had been like this ever since he was a toddler, when he was always on the move. He climbed out of his cot, escaped out of the house, seemed to have little sense of danger, and was a terror to take to the supermarket or to visit friends. He was always forgetting where he had put things, and often seemed to act without thinking and blurted out silly things in company.

Alan's parents had tried everything: special diets, remedial teaching and a special tutor, punishments and counselling. Now that he was an adolescent, he was becoming hard to discipline at school and impossible at home: hence the referral.

Alan had a condition called Attention Deficit Disorder. This is sometimes referred to as ADD. Not all children with this disorder are as overactive and restless as Alan, but if they are, the disorder is called Attention Deficit Hyperactivity Disorder (ADHD). There have been a number of other names for this in the past, and not all doctors or psychiatrists or psychologists have agreed that the condition exists at all. We have learnt a lot about the condition in recent years however, and now recognize that it occurs quite commonly, perhaps affecting one or two children in every hundred, perhaps even more. Some children are more severely affected than others.

ADD is not due to mental illness or intellectual disability. It can occur in highly intelligent people, but it can make it very hard for them to learn at school and very hard for their teachers to cope with. It probably results from an imbalance in one of the chemical substances in the brain called neurotransmitters that regulate how messages pass from one nerve cell to another. It is suggested that one of these neurotransmitters has the job of selecting which messages should get through and which should be disregarded. We all see and hear so many things from the world around us, and we are capable of so many thoughts and ideas, that we need to be able to concentrate on the task in hand and pay no attention to anything that is not really important.

This seems to be the problem for children with ADD, whose minds are constantly switching from one thing to another. No matter how hard they try to focus on their work, they are constantly being distracted by little things like a passing car, a dropped pencil or another child, so that their school work and attempts to study are interrupted every few minutes. No wonder they have difficulty in keeping still, trouble in paying attention, and tend to distract others around them.

WHAT ARE THE FEATURES OF ADD?

Not all children with ADD will have all the features of this condition. One would hope, of course, that by the time a child has reached secondary school and is a teenager, ADD will be recognized and treatment will have been started. Unfortunately this is not always so, particularly as several other conditions in childhood can be very like ADD and make it difficult to diagnose. It is possible to have both ADD and another condition such as a learning disability as well, and this may have delayed the diagnosis.

If children with ADD have reached adolescence without the disorder being recognized, there is a risk that they will have had so many set-backs at school, and perhaps gained such a bad reputation, that it will have become much more complicated and harder to resolve. Teenagers in this situation may have given up trying, feeling everyone is blaming them for something that they can't help.

Here are some of the features of ADD. He or she (but usually it is he):

- Fidgets, squirms and feels restless
- Finds it hard to stay seated (but this may become easier after puberty)
- Is easily distracted
- Can't pay attention for more than a few minutes
- Interrupts, intrudes on other conversations
- Distracts other students in the classroom
- Talks excessively
- Doesn't seem to listen: tends to interrupt
- Fails to complete tasks (starts but can't finish)
- Shifts from one incompleted task to another
- Blurts out answers to questions apparently without thought
- Can't wait to take turns
- Inconsistent performance at school
- Acts before thinking: impulsive
- Is not easily satisfied: won't take no for an answer
- Loses things
- Has a poor sense of danger
- Overwhelms friends, may irritate other people

These features will have been present from an early age, and certainly before the age of 7. A child with ADD will be difficult both at home and at school, but his behaviour will be worse when he is in a group (such as at school), and the problem will be less obvious when he is with just one person.

Usually by teenage, if untreated, ADD will have led to considerable difficulties in learning and school behaviour.

Of course, most children and teenagers have some of these characteristics to some extent. Perhaps it won't worry some, and in others they only cause a problem at times.

Whether a child could be given the diagnosis of ADD or just has the signs of a very active boy may depend to some extent on how severe the problem is and how much distress it is causing the family, the school and the child himself.

ADD CAN BE HELPED BY TREATMENT

Parents who suspect that their child or teenager may have ADD should discuss this with their child's teachers and their doctor. It may be necessary to do some tests to make sure that there is not some other problem that could affect learning. Treatment should be a cooperative effort between paediatrician, teacher and parents (and of course the teenager himself, who will need to understand the nature of the problem and the reasons for treatment). The most helpful aspect of treatment is medication, but this alone is usually not enough.

Alan had some tests to check on his learning skills. He had a full physical check and had an opportunity to tell me what he felt his problems were, and what he would like changed. It turned out that despite his bad reputation at school, he really did want to learn and to stay at school. So far it was just too difficult for him.

The school was most cooperative in helping Alan, who started a simple form of medication. Improvement started at once, both in behaviour and in the way he was able to study in the classroom. He was quite proud of the school reports that he brought to show me.

CHAPTER 6

MUSIC
AND PARTIES

Loud music: feels good, but does it harm?

It's bad enough when teenagers turn on their radio or play their tapes in their room and the whole house is subjected to the throb and beat of their music. It doesn't matter whether you like it or not (you probably can't stand it), you can't get away from it or ignore it. It's worse, in some ways, when you can't actually hear the music but you can feel the beat coming through the headphones of their Walkman when you are standing several metres away. If you can hear or feel it from that distance, what must it sound like with the headphones clamped to their ears? What is it doing to their hearing?

WHY DO TEENAGERS LIKE THEIR MUSIC SO LOUD?

Teenagers really feel their music. It turns them on. It provides atmosphere at a party. It reminds them of the excitement of a concert, with its lights, and the mass of other teenagers, and the beat and movement and sexual overtones. It is like a drug: it gives them a high. It gives them a common bond: they can feel (or imagine) that they are part of a group, whether they are at a party or a disco or just by themselves at home. It's repetitive, and that's comforting. It's anti-parent, and that's cool. It helps them identify with the band or the singer. It gives them something to talk about with their friends. It's their music. It's their scene.

Now all this only really works if the music is loud. The louder the better — when it really gets into you, when you feel that you are immersed in it. This may not be true for all teenagers, of course. Some just enjoy their music, and like it loud to appreciate it.

DOES LOUD MUSIC CAUSE HARM?

You might argue that this drug-like effect of loud music is better than getting high on alcohol, or stoned on marijuana. So it is perhaps, except that drugs are often combined with the music, to enhance the great feeling it gives.

The question is: does loud music do harm to the ears or to hearing?

The answer is that it can and does. Studies from the National Acoustic Laboratories have shown that teenagers and young adults are showing hearing loss at a rate that wouldn't normally occur until they were much older. Everyone's hearing tends to become less acute with increasing age. It should be very acute during the teen years and in the twenties and thirties. Normally, it isn't until people get quite old, perhaps in their eighties, that you have to repeat yourself when you want to talk to them, and they might need hearing-aids to understand ordinary conversation.

Now, in an age of deafening rock and high-powered stereos and headphones, young people are losing their hearing at almost three times the rate that they used to. Not only that, but there may be obvious and irreparable damage to hearing before the age of 30 in those who have regularly listened to loud music. It's much worse for singers and players in a band.

The first signs of impending damage that someone may notice is ringing in the ears. This will probably be temporary at first, and last only a short time after listening to loud music. Later it lasts longer and may persist. After this, there is difficulty in distinguishing speech in a noisy room, or from the back seat of the car. Later still, sounds become muffled and conversation seems faint or blurry. People with damaged hearing will miss sounds that other people can hear. They will say 'Speak up, you're mumbling' when they really mean that their hearing is going.

The alarming thing is that all this is happening now, not just in the elderly, but in young people in their late teens and in their twenties.

HOW MUCH NOISE CAN CAUSE DAMAGE TO HEARING?

This depends on the degree of loudness and how long the teenager listens to it. In general, really loud music can have a bad effect in a matter of a few hours. A tape on headphones playing at 100 decibels could cause damage in one evening, but it is the repeated exposure that is a risk for permanent damage.

All teenagers who hear ringing in their ears after listening to loud music are running a real risk of causing hearing damage. They should at least be told about the risk. Some will reduce the sound and save their ears. Some will decide that the loud music is worth the risk.

MUSIC WHILE STUDYING

'My teenager is doing Year 10 this year. It's a very important year, and she must do as well as she can. She's passing, but when she does her homework, she insists on having her dreadful music blaring away. I don't know how she could concentrate. Should I take her cassette player from her in school term?'

'Mum, why don't you listen to me when I tell you that I can't study when there's no music? I don't really listen to it. I actually study better with the music playing.'

'Then why don't you play nice soft music?' (I suspect the mother meant her own sort of music, and said this for her own sanity.)

'Firstly it's really boring music, and secondly, it's so horrible that I couldn't study against it. I'd keep hearing it.'

Despite what you might expect, some teenagers actually do study better when there is a background of music. They don't really hear it most of the time, but it's a supportive background to their thinking, and it may be an aid to study. Just make sure that it isn't too noisy: it shouldn't disturb the others in the house, and if it is really loud it will certainly interfere with learning.

Some teenagers, on the other hand, will be listening to music *instead* of studying, just to pass the time. They need some firm advice, and maybe threats to remove the cassette player or radio during homework hours.

Teenage parties

Teenage parties can be a big worry to parents. What will teenagers do? Will there be alcohol? What about drugs? Should you make a firm time for your teenager to come home? Should you pick up your teenager after the party, even if your teenager says she would die from embarrassment? Can you trust the boy she is going with?

Parties have always been a part of teenage social life. However much parents may worry about what goes on at some parties, it's even worse if teenagers don't get asked at all. Most teenagers are completely trustworthy, and most realize that their parents won't really relax until they return home. Even for them it is helpful to make some rules: it gives them guidelines for what you expect, and if there is pressure from friends to do something that they feel is wrong, they can always blame their very unreasonable parents when they refuse.

For other teenagers, there may be a risk that they will get carried away by the rest of the group. It is natural to want to be part of the group, and not left out. Parties can be an escape from family and their boring evenings, so let's have some real fun. What parents don't know about what goes on at the party can't hurt them. When you are having fun, what the hell?

The dangers for some teenagers, especially for 15 to 18 year olds, are excess alcohol, drugs and unwanted sex. The worry is getting home safely. If parents can resolve these issues, they can rest easy for the night.

WHAT ARE REASONABLE RULES?

Rules obviously vary according to the age of the teenager and the extent to which the party is supervised. The following guidelines apply to most teenagers going to a party.

Make sure you know where your teenager is going, and make sure there is a contact phone number. If there is a change in venue, make sure he or she lets you know by phone.

Will there be adults present? Do you know them? If your teenager is young, it is a good idea to phone the parents of the friend giving the party so you know who they are. Offer help if this seems appropriate, particularly in backing them up if they are imposing rules about when the party finishes or alcohol.

If you are also going out yourself, make sure that your teenager knows where you are and how they could reach you by phone.

Agree on the question of alcohol. Will there be alcohol at the party? If you think that your teenager will drink, and you accept this, set limits. If you disapprove, make sure that they know this. If your teenager is underage and tells you everyone drinks at parties, tell them that it isn't true. Lots of teenagers choose *not* to drink, and still have a good time and don't lose their friends.

Agree on a time to return home. Make sure your teenager knows that if anything happens that may make them late, they must phone to tell you.

Make sure that you know exactly how your teenager is going to get home. A lift from a friend is not good enough unless you know the friend, and know that they are reliable, and if the friend is young, that they don't drink when they are going to drive.

Make sure that your teenager has the money for a phone call and, if necessary, for a taxi.

Be prepared to wait up for your teenager, or at least wake up when they return. Tell your teenager to come in to say goodnight if you have already gone to bed.

YOUR TEENAGER IS GIVING THE PARTY — IN YOUR HOUSE

Same rules apply. Decide about alcohol, and if you decide against it make sure everyone coming to the party knows about it well in advance. If you meet with resistance from your teenager, phone around their friends' parents: you'll probably find that they will back you all the way.

No drugs. Anyone who brings drugs is asked to leave.

Be around. Resist the invitation to go out and leave the young in peace to do their own thing. Appear from time to time (but don't hang around all the time — you'd be bored to death). If they are making too much noise, say so. You may need to warn the neighbours.

The bedrooms are off limits.

When the agreed time for the party to finish comes, stand by it. Remember the suffering neighbours and the worried parents of your teenager's friends.

CHAPTER 7

THE NUTS AND BOLTS OF TEENAGE SEX

On being fertile

I'd known Tina for some years, as I had been looking after her diabetes. She was now 15 and came to see me without her mother. She didn't waste time with preliminaries, which meant she was worried. 'Can you tell me if I'm pregnant?'

It turned out that her last period had been six weeks ago, and her boyfriend hadn't used a condom. He was quite a lot older than she was, and at 15, it was understandable that she didn't want her mother to know about her worries concerning pregnancy. But she was living at home and going to school, and certainly needed her family's support for this and a lot of other things in her life.

Fortunately the pregnancy test was negative. It gave us both an opportunity to discuss contraception, Pap smears and how she really felt

about this relationship. She ended up bringing her mother into the discussion and making an appointment to see her family doctor.

Children have an interest and excitement about sex from an early age and this becomes much stronger during puberty. Sexual development, both the physical as well as the psychological and social aspects, is a rather gradual process, culminating in the teenager's ability to reproduce. Whereas most children are ready and waiting for their sexual development (unless it comes much too early), and most seem to cope well with their sexual feelings, they are not ready to become parents.

People become fertile and able to reproduce in their mid-teens. A girl is capable of becoming pregnant when she ovulates. This is when mature ova are released from the ovaries so they can become impregnated by sperm. A boy is capable of fertilizing a girl when he can ejaculate sperm. For most boys and girls, these events occur before their fourteenth birthday.

Ejaculation in boys, and menstruation and ovulation in girls, come long before they have finished schooling, long before they are emotionally mature, long before they are ready to give up normal teenage social life, long before they are financially independent, and long before they can expect to form a stable or lasting relationship in which to raise a child. This is not true for people growing up in some societies — where teenage marriages are the norm and well accepted, and girls are not expected to get further education — but it is certainly true for people growing up in Western societies.

Intercourse

In 1992 a large survey of Australian secondary school students, from ages 12 to 16, found that by age 16 (Year 11 students), 38% of boys and 36% of girls had had sex ('gone all the way'). At age 14, 20% of boys and 10% of girls had had sex. Even at age 12, 8% of boys and 2% of girls had had sex. Most had had sex with only one partner, and most had used condoms.

Another survey suggested that 53% of teenagers think that it is alright to have sex, provided it is with a steady partner; 91% of the girls and 69% of boys said that it is not acceptable to have sex with more than one partner.

American studies have shown that in most teenage pregnancies the father is an older man, often someone who has left school and in his early twenties.

The good news about all this, however, is that most teenagers are not having sexual intercourse. Those that do are not promiscuous, but have sex within a single relationship (relationships change of course, but it suggests that sex has been a part of the relationship, rather than just for the sake of sex). Most sexually active teenagers use condoms.

But there are still many girls at risk of becoming pregnant.

AHEM··· WELL FIRST OF ALL·· AH··· AHEM THEN···· ··· WELL··· ·· AH···

Parents need to know that teenagers tend to be influenced by each other's expectations, and that they live in a teenage society where sex is generally approved within a close relationship.

Sexual orientation

Peter was aged 14 and had been brought by his mother because he was unhappy and refused to talk to anyone about it. His father was disgusted with him. He was not speaking to him since a gay magazine had been found under Peter's mattress when his mother was spring-cleaning his room.

When Peter had a chance to talk alone, he confirmed how miserable he was. He had thought of killing himself, but felt he hadn't the guts to do it properly. He was very upset about the gay magazine being found. He thought he was probably gay and he knew exactly what his father felt about it.

As children enter puberty, their interest in sex awakens and sexual urges can be quite powerful. At this stage most children still prefer the company of children of the same sex. Naturally they share some of their sexual curiosity and excitement together: perhaps boys more so than girls. They are interested in each other's sexual development. They may speculate, at least privately, about what their friends do and what they think about. Although the boys' talk will be mainly about girls, it isn't just girls that excite them at this stage. Almost any thought about sex, including each other's, will excite them.

It is not surprising therefore that some boys (and girls) may wonder about their sexual feelings, and may be worried when they find they become sexually aroused by thinking about other teenagers of the same sex. This is quite common, and it has been estimated that about 10% of boys are confused about their sexual orientation. This means that many young teenagers worry that they may be gay.

It may not be quite such a worry for girls, for a number of reasons. One of these is that girls can touch and hug each other without anyone being surprised or feeling that it is wrong. If boys hug or kiss each other, it certainly leads to a lot of comment. They can embrace on the sporting field if someone kicks a goal at football, but this is certainly not a loving or caring gesture, as it may be in girls. Boys cannot show this kind of physical affection towards each other, even though they may be really good friends and enjoy each other's company.

This is really just an attitude of our Western, modern-day society. It is not universal, and some societies allow boys to show physical affection, hold hands in company without embarrassment, just as girls do. There have been times when homosexual behaviour between young teenagers was thought to be natural and just a passing phase in their sexual development.

Boys tend to show considerable fear and distaste towards gay youth. It is not entirely clear why they do so. It may be that many are just a bit unsure of their own sexual feelings. It may be they really feel disgusted at the thought of sexual acts between males. Whatever the reason, if a boy is thought to be gay by his peers, it is likely that he will have a very bad time from them. And this is on top of his own confusion, perhaps guilt, and fear that his parents will find out.

As teenagers mature in their personal development, most of the confusion about their sexual feelings will be resolved. Most of those who worried about whether they might be gay, will find that they do develop an interest in girls, and are aroused by the thought of sexual intercourse. Some may still feel sexually excited by both boys and girls. A small number, perhaps 1%, will realize that they are mainly attracted by people of the same sex, and are truly gay. Some of these will need a lot of help in sorting out their feelings, in how to tell their friends, and particularly their parents.

There is still some argument about whether children are born with their sexual orientation already decided by genetic factors. People may be 'born gay'. Perhaps there are other factors, including early life experiences. Whatever the cause, it is certain that it is not the teenager's fault if they are gay, and although there are decisions they must make about what they do sexually, there is probably nothing that can be done to make a gay teenager straight.

TALKING ABOUT SEXUAL FEELINGS

It may be hard for parents to help their teenager sort out his or her sexual feelings. It tends to cause embarrassment all round. But if parents do feel comfortable in talking about sex with their teenager, and if the teenager wants to talk about this with their parents, they should certainly do so. Ideally they should start talking about sex long before puberty, of course, and this makes it easier to continue talking about it later.

If there does seem to be a difficulty for the teenager in sorting out his or her feelings, it is often better to involve some adult outside the family, such as an understanding doctor, or youth worker or counsellor. It would be unfair to regard the young person as having a mental illness, so that although a child psychiatrist or psychologist would be very competent at advising about sexual orientation, it might be best to involve one mainly if there are associated emotional concerns.

The best way to help a young teenager with their confused sexuality is to make it clear that you are happy to talk about it if they would like. If not, you can find someone who could help. Whatever turns out, it won't affect your pride and love for your teenage child, and that is very important to them, and you may have to reassure them about this quite often.

Peter wanted to talk about his sexual feelings, about how guilty he felt about feeling gay, and how he felt he had let his parents down by feeling this way. On the one hand he wanted to share his sexual feelings with other gay youth (in the same way that most youth start looking for a girlfriend), but found this impossible, and on the other he felt so guilty about his sexual urges, that he wanted to avoid sex and be thought of as 'normal'.

Surprisingly, perhaps, it didn't

seem to upset his mother too much to know that he was gay. She just felt so much better that Peter was feeling happier. His father still wanted me to make him heterosexual, and insisted it was just a stage, but at least he started to speak to Peter again. And Peter felt better that he didn't have to hide his feelings any more from his parents.

Masturbation: must you?

When a teenager says 'Can I ask you a personal question?', it's nearly always about sexual feelings or behaviour. It is usually asked at the end of a consultation when everything seems to have been covered and time has run out. But it takes some courage for a teenager to raise a subject such as sex with an adult, so however much I am rushed for time, I try to respect the teenager's wish to discuss something as private and potentially embarrassing as this. At home it will probably come up at the most inconvenient times too, but if we put off discussing a sensitive question that is bothering a young person, he or she probably won't bring it up again and the opportunity may be lost.

I had known Paul for a few weeks. He had lots of problems that weighed heavily on his mind: he wasn't very popular, he wasn't very tall, he thought he would never be attractive to girls. We had looked into the fact that he was rather short and somewhat late coming into puberty (which probably accounted for his lack of confidence socially: he had been teased by some of the boys, and shunned by some of the girls at his school).

His personal question, asked at the end of a meeting, was: 'Do you think I may be oversexed?' His real concern was that he might be masturbating far too often, and he wanted to know how often was normal. He wondered whether he may be doing himself psychological harm.

I don't suppose anyone believes now that masturbation could possibly cause physical harm. Many years ago (perhaps not so long ago really, and maybe within a parent's memory) people really thought that it was not only morally bad but that it could make you go mad or become a criminal. That seems really absurd, especially as most people holding those views must have done it themselves in their own youth.

This view was based partly on the observation that people in mental asylums, who were watched closely by their guardians and nurses, were seen to masturbate: not surprising, as the inmates had no other sexual outlet, they didn't know it was so wrong, and they had no privacy. The conclusion was reached that it was the masturbation that had made them go insane. The same was true for prisoners in gaol, and the conclusion was reached that it was masturbation that made them turn to crime. It was only men who were observed to masturbate, so it was thought that it was a male vice. This is of course laughable, but the view was held by respectable physicians, priests, teachers and parents until quite recently.

Even if masturbation wasn't thought to cause physical harm, it was thought by many to be immoral and shameful. Most teenagers would be mortified if their parents caught them masturbating, and many would be horrified if their friends actually saw them doing it. Why is so much made of something that everyone now agrees is harmless and normal and almost universal?

Young infants often get pleasure from rubbing their genitals. They tend to lose interest after a while as they begin to explore the world around them and find so many other things to excite and interest them. Their early experience however may have some lasting effect if a parent finds them doing it and punishes or shames them. They quickly learn that there is something bad about touching their genitals, and any pleasure they get is forbidden or shameful.

Later in childhood masturbation is less common, though interest and excitement about sex is never lost. With puberty, sexual feelings increase in direct proportion to the stage of puberty, and in boys at least (in whom research studies have been made) the greater amount of the male hormone testosterone that is circulating in the body, the more often the adolescent will masturbate or have other sexual activities.

Girls masturbate too, of course, though some studies suggest that fewer do so and probably less often than boys. There has been much more written in recent years about girls' sexuality, and so much published in popular magazines, that it is likely that girls will feel more comfortable about this than they used to.

WHAT IS NORMAL?

So, coming back to Paul's question: how often is too much, and what is normal? Can someone do any harm to themselves by frequent masturbation? Could a boy waste sperm? Could a boy find it harder to have proper sex with a girl if he masturbates too often? Could it mean that he was really homosexual?

The answers to all these questions are reassuring. A person can't harm himself or herself by masturbating. Many people masturbate every day and often several times a day. A boy can't waste sperm, as the testes make millions of sperm every day, year after year. The amount of semen will decrease temporarily if ejaculation occurs very often, but the volume quickly increases after a few days. Masturbating does not mean that a boy is homosexual. Nor does it in any way make it more difficult to have intercourse later.

There is one proviso: if a teenager is actually worried about their sexual behaviour, including masturbation, it may be helpful to have an opportunity to sort out these feelings, if not with a parent, then with a professional advisor. Otherwise they may get a lot of mis-information from friends and magazines, which could make them even more confused.

There is another point to make: it is not compulsory to masturbate. Lots of teenagers hardly ever do, for a variety of reasons. Maybe they have tried it once or twice and it didn't feel good. Maybe they are saving their sexual experience for a close relationship later on. Maybe they just don't feel the urge. It's perfectly normal to feel this way also.

Could you get 'addicted' to masturbation? Any pleasurable activity, including eating and jogging for instance, can become such a part of life and such a source of comfort and pleasure, that a teenager might want to do it a lot, and feel bad when they can't. This can be true for masturbation, but it is not an addiction, and is not necessarily harmful unless it interferes with other activities — in that case, it is worthwhile seeking professional help.

Coming back to Paul's worry. After he had discussed his concerns, and had felt relieved about his worst fears, he found he was more relaxed about his sexual urges, was masturbating less often and looking forward to his first sexual experience within a close relationship with a girl.

CHAPTER 8

NUTRITION, DIETS AND BODY SHAPE

Good nutrition, bad diets

Teenagers don't always eat the kinds of food that their parents would like them to. Perhaps it was never easy to get them to eat all their vegetables when they were younger, but now it's almost impossible. They either eat the family out of food with their constant raids on the fridge, or they reject most of the good nutrition provided at the table. They have no time for breakfast, but don't stop eating when they come home from school. Despite all this, they seem healthy enough. But could they be harming their future health? What about calcium? Iron? Vitamins? Salt? Are they risking heart disease in later life? Diabetes? High blood pressure? Osteoporosis-weak bones?

Several things influence adolescent eating patterns. Some teenagers are probably at greater risk than others, but most are at no real risk at all, at least as far as their immediate health is concerned.

TEENAGERS BURN UP MUCH MORE ENERGY IN PHYSICAL ACTIVITY AND THEY NEED MORE FOOD FOR THEIR RAPID GROWTH

Adolescents need more energy (calories, or kilojoules) from their food than at any other time of life. They need this partly for growth, but even during the rapid growth spurt, the needs for growth don't fully account for their enormous appetites. Teenagers burn up a great deal of energy on physical activity. They have so much bigger bodies to push around, it is not surprising that it takes more fuel to do it.

One study of 16 year olds in Australia showed that the average number of calories boys took in from food was over 3000 calories (12,600 kilojoules), and the average intake for girls was over 2000 calories (8400 kilojoules). Many ate far more than this average amount. This seems a lot, and it is. Teenagers are expensive to feed. The same study showed that almost a third of their calories came from snacks, the rest from the main meals.

Of course there is a wide variation from one adolescent to another. The variation depends on their rate of growth, their stage of puberty and their level of physical activity. Growth is not just in height, but in the way the body broadens out, and develops more muscle and fat. Physical activity isn't just sport and exercise, but fidgeting and general body movement.

FAT TEENAGERS DON'T ALWAYS EAT MORE THAN SLIM ONES

Many teenagers, particularly girls, put on weight as fat in the early years of puberty. Some may have been a bit (or even a lot) overweight since early childhood, but it seems to stack on at puberty. Although many overweight teenagers do eat more than they need, they usually don't eat more than teenagers who are not fat. Most mothers with a slim, active teenage boy would agree that he eats more than his overweight sisters. 'You can't fill him.' Of course all teenagers eat junk food and sweets sometimes, but if they are fat, they get blamed for it.

EATING IS A SOCIAL ACTIVITY FOR TEENAGERS

Eating is one of the things that teenagers like to do together. The most readily available foods are fast-foods like hamburgers, chips, cola drinks and sweets. This is no coincidence: the fast-food outlets have carefully market-researched teenagers' likes and have gone all-out to supply them. One advantage is that these foods tend to be high in food energy, so they help meet the teenager's need for plenty of high-energy foods. It is a disadvantage, of course, for overweight teenagers, as it means that all their favourite social foods make it very difficult for them to control their weight.

APPETITE IS USUALLY THE BEST JUDGE OF HOW MUCH TEENAGERS NEED TO EAT

For most teenagers, their appetite makes sure that they get the right amount of food. Their appetite will vary quite a lot from day to day, depending on what is served up for dinner, or how busy they are after school. In general, things balance out over a period of about 10 days. If they eat a lot over a few days, they usually eat less over the next few days, so their weight remains fairly consistent with growth.

This control of weight seems to be under the control of a part of the brain which determines appetite and hunger. It also tells us when we have had enough. It works well so long as we listen to its messages. The same area of the brain monitors how much we eat of different foods. This makes sure that we get a variety of different foods, and thus get enough vitamins and minerals and proteins and other essential foods.

It works this way: a teenager might eat a

SOME THINGS OVERRIDE THIS CONTROL SYSTEM OF NATURE

The 'appetite' control system works very well for most healthy young people. It is well suited to active teenagers who have access to a variety of good foods when they are at home and when they are out socially. But things can override the control system, particularly in our Western, affluent society.

1. Fast foods, sweets and soft drinks

These can be very seductive for some people. They tend to be very attractive and high in energy, so they provide a lot of calories without filling people up. They are also used as social foods rather than as foods to satisfy nutrition.

2. Inactivity

By nature, human beings are meant to be active. This burns up excess calories and allows the teenager's natural drive for food to be balanced out. But if a teenager is not very active, the balance may become disturbed, and food intake exceeds energy output. Some studies in America have shown that the more hours children spend watching television each day, the fatter they tend to become.

3. Boredom

Teenagers don't take kindly to boredom. If they have nothing to do, their thoughts might turn to food. Eating then becomes a source of pleasure, of something to do. Naturally this runs the risk of accumulating too many calories.

4. Emotional disturbance

Strong emotions can override nature's best efforts to keep things in balance. We all tend to lose our appetite if we are very upset. Some people eat more when they are depressed or under stress. So do teenagers, and if the emotional disturbance is sustained for any length of time, the body's energy balance may become disturbed too.

5. Fear of becoming fat

Some teenagers are so worried about being fat (even if they aren't) that they diet excessively. This may be the basis of anorexia nervosa. In this condition we believe that psychological factors override the body's weight control mechanism, and fear of putting on weight may be stronger than the body's natural drive to eat.

6. Illness

Some illnesses interfere with appetite, or may prevent food being properly absorbed from the gut or used by the body. Examples include diabetes (before it is diagnosed and treatment starts), severe asthma, and certain bowel disorders. Some hormonal disturbances, such as thyroid disease, also interfere with weight control and energy balance.

lot of one kind of favourite food, and after a while get sick of it and switch to a different food. A teenager might have filled himself or herself up with meat and potatoes at dinner, but can easily find room for fruit or dessert. The result is that he or she gets a variety of foods.

VITAMINS, MINERALS AND FIBRE

It is of course not enough to consider just how much a teenager is eating. It may be that there is a lack of certain essential components of food, such as vitamins or minerals. Sometimes there may be too much of certain constituents, such as salt or fat. There may be a lack of food fibre which is needed for normal bowel function.

The fact is, however, that provided a teenager is having plenty of good foods it is extremely unlikely that there will be any deficiencies of essential vitamins or minerals. It is only if they seem to be avoiding many foods, or have placed themselves on a special diet, that you may need to consider these elements of their nutrition.

Calcium

Many foods contain calcium. Teenagers need a good intake of calcium to develop healthy bones. People lay down about 40% of their bone mass during adolescence, and this stands them in good stead throughout life.

Most of a child's and teenager's calcium comes from milk and other dairy produce such as cheese and yogurt. If your teenager is having plenty of these foods, don't worry. If not, they may be getting enough calcium from other foods such as Milo, soya, pizza with cheese, sardines, shellfish, sesame seeds, treacle, parsley and spinach.

Iron

Boys and girls need a good supply of iron in their food during adolescence. They are expanding their blood system as they grow, and boys especially are developing higher levels of haemoglobin (the red substance in blood cells, which helps oxygen to be carried around the body in the bloodstream). Girls need more iron when they start menstruating, so they can replace the blood lost in the menstrual period. Studies show that most teenage boys have plenty of iron in their diet, but many girls get barely enough, and some develop a deficiency, which may lead to anaemia.

Foods that contain iron include red meat, spinach, Milo and Ovaltine, bran, yeast, muesli, nuts and sesame seeds, and curry.

Vitamins

Teenagers who have a mixed diet with a range of foods are not likely to develop a vitamin deficiency. There is plenty of the Vitamin B group in wholemeal cereals and bread, yeast, Milo and Ovaltine, soya, nuts and some meats. Vegemite is very rich in the B group.

Vitamin C is plentiful in fruits, juices and vegetables (including potato). It can be destroyed by excessive cooking and exposure to air, but most teenagers get plenty.

Fibre

Dietary fibre comes from whole grains, wholemeal bread, cereals, beans, dried fruits, and fresh fruit and vegetables, but not animal products such as milk or meat. We don't know how much fibre is really needed to maintain health, but it has been shown that a good intake of fibre can lead to healthy bowel function. Whether fibre helps prevent disease in later life is not yet proven.

Salt

Salt is essential for life. Many people are worried that the large amount of salt that teenagers take, especially in snacks and take-away foods, will cause high blood pressure. Only a proportion of the population have difficulty in handling salt, but those that do are more likely to get high blood pressure (hypertension) if they eat more salt than they need.

Many foods naturally contain salt, and this is really enough for most of us. The extra salt that is eaten comes from salt added in cooking and food preparation, and salt taken at the table.

Teenagers usually don't really need this added salt, though it probably doesn't harm the majority of them. However, it's better to get used to little or no added salt, because the more you add salt to food, the more you feel you need to make the food taste good. Then, for those young people liable to get hypertension, it becomes a problem.

High blood pressure tends to run in families. If either parent has high blood pressure, it would be wise for all the family to cut down their salt intake, and get used to low-salt cooking.

WHEN SHOULD A PARENT START TO WORRY ABOUT A TEENAGER'S NUTRITION?

Parents seldom need to worry about their child's nutrition, even when their food intake seems really weird and abnormal. They do, however, need to have some concern if:

- Their teenager is losing weight steadily and to the point of becoming underweight.

- Their teenager is gaining weight steadily, and out of proportion to growth, and to the point of becoming fat.

- Their teenager has decided to put herself on a strange diet, and is avoiding certain foods without discussing this with you. She might have become a vegetarian without thinking how she will get enough protein or iron or calories.

- Their teenager is having a lot of stomach pains and constipation.

If you are worried about any of these things, it is worth discussing it with your family doctor. Sometimes a dietitian may be able to reassure you that your teenager is getting all the essential nutrients he or she needs. Sometimes teenagers may need to change their eating habits a bit to make sure they are getting balanced nutrition.

DIETS ARE SELDOM HELPFUL EXCEPT FOR MEDICAL CONDITIONS

Remember: unless your teenager has a chronic illness for which a special diet has been prescribed, there is seldom any advantage (and often many disadvantages) in putting him or her on a diet. Teenagers seldom stick to diets, and diets seldom do teenagers much good. And this often makes them feel guilty, and leads to family arguments and frustration.

The best advice for a parent is to give plenty of healthy foods that the family likes, and to make sure there is a good variety. If the teenager goes and eats unsuitable foods as snacks, think of these as extras: you have provided the basic needs.

Teenagers who think they are too fat

'Look at me. It's disgusting. I'm fat. It's obvious. Here, on my stomach. Here, on my hips. Look at my arms. I hate it.'

Linda prodded away at her stomach and hips in disgust. She refused to believe that her parents or I had any idea what it was to be fat, as none of us thought she was even slightly overweight. Either that, or we were too polite to tell her.

'What do your friends say?' I asked.

'Oh yeah. As if they'd tell me I was fat.'

'Perhaps they don't think that you are fat. I bet most of them are heavier than you.'

'None of them. They are all skinny. I'm so ashamed.'

'All of them are thinner than you?'

'Well, there's one girl. But she's gross. And she's the only one.'

This unsatisfactory conversation could have gone on for some time, as it was clear that measurements of weight and height, with comparison with the normal growth charts, weren't going to persuade Linda that she wasn't overweight. What she saw in the mirror was what she was. And it didn't measure up too well against the pictures in Cosmopolitan *and* Cleo *or the models in advertisements or the girls on the TV shows . . .*

A high proportion of girls in our society consider themselves as too fat. This is true throughout teenage. In a survey of Year 9 girls, for example, 53% of normal-weight girls, in addition to 93% of overweight girls, thought they were fat; 8% of thin girls thought they were overweight. Thus, when we compare what they feel about their body shape with actual measurements of their weight compared to their height, we find that many perfectly normal-weight girls, and some very underweight girls, still think of themselves as fat.

Why is this so? Adolescents have always been very interested, some would say preoccupied, with their bodies. The problem is that they are always comparing their body with others. Not just their friends, but young adults whom they admire. Models, TV characters, sporting heroes, girls in magazine advertisements, film stars. And in recent decades, in Western society, these people have tended to be slim. They are often selected because of this, particularly as men are supposed to admire slim women. Whether this is so or not, there is no doubt that well-rounded women, even fat women, seem to have no trouble in finding a male partner and getting happily married. But this fact carries no weight at all with teenage girls. They *know* that boys like slim girls.

Fat boys get a bad time, too. They tend to get harassed by other kids, especially kids they don't know or boys in other grades at school. Even boys in the same grade at school, who should be their friends, may tease them sometimes.

So it is not surprising that teenagers want to be slim. And it is not surprising that most teenagers would really like to be just a bit thinner. Or a lot thinner.

This is particularly true for girls, but in the survey of Victorian teenagers, 12% of normal-weight boys in Year 9 thought they were too fat. Only half the number of overweight boys thought of themselves as fat. One difference between boys and girls was that no underweight boy in the survey thought he was fat, but 8% of underweight girls thought of themselves as being too fat.

WHAT CAN YOU DO IF YOUR TEENAGE DAUGHTER THINKS SHE IS TOO FAT (BUT YOU DON'T, AND SHE ISN'T)?

You can't do much to stop her worrying. It's natural to worry about body shape, so long as it doesn't take up too much of her time worrying, and it doesn't get her down too much.

You need to reassure her, of course, lots of times. She needs good clothes that she can feel proud of herself in. She needs reassurance from her friends (often more convincing than her parents, because she knows her parents love her no matter how hideous she is, and wouldn't hurt her feelings, but she can trust her friends to say what they think). She could do with a good friendship with a boy who admires her, perhaps.

DON'T ALLOW HER TO DIET

You can't dismiss her worries as stupid. They may be real worries and they can cause real misery at times. So you listen to her concerns about her weight. You then work out a health plan that includes some exercise each day and good food. You do not allow a diet of any kind. A good meal plan means having three meals a day with healthy snacks between meals.

SUSTAIN HER SELF-ESTEEM

Thinking that she is fat will only really get her down if she feels generally bad about herself. If she is popular, or good at sport, or drama or art, and has plenty of self-confidence, she probably won't get into any trouble, and will put thoughts of being fat into perspective. Most of the time she will forget about it. Unfortunately being smart at schoolwork doesn't always seem to give a teenager the same protection. Perhaps this is because success in school isn't the most popular characteristic for a young teenager, at a time when she is striving to be like her peers and hoping for their approval.

So the best thing that parents can do may be to build up her strengths and self-confidence. They don't need to deny her weight problem (or what she thinks is a problem), but they can put it into perspective so it seems less important.

Linda decided to take 20 minutes a day doing some exercise like taking the family dog for a walk. She would work on tightening up her stomach muscles rather than concentrating on the frustrating task of actually losing weight. Her mother went shopping with her and together they found really great clothes that, to her surprise, she fitted into and looked good in. She had some of her friends over for the night. They talked about boys, and no-one seemed to mention her weight.

On being really fat

Our society plays a heavy price for not having to do much hard physical work to get plenty of food. Of course it's infinitely better to have plenty of good food than not having enough like a very large part of the world's population. Not only is the food plentiful, but it is high in energy content. That is good for some of us, and not so good for a lot of us.

During adolescence, many people get overweight. This is more true for girls, but increasing numbers of boys are also fat. It is a worry for them, because it is not well thought of by other teenagers, or by people in general. It is also a worry, because many overweight teenagers stay overweight as adults. It is also a worry because efforts to lose weight usually end in failure, no matter how hard the teenager tries. And to make it worse, being fat is seldom the fault of the teenager, yet he or she will get blamed for it, more often than not.

Most people think that fat people are greedy and eat too much. There are many reasons why people are the build they are, whether they are thin or fat. It is not fair or rational to assume that all overweight teenagers have the same problem, or that they necessarily have a problem at all.

THE MOST USUAL FORM OF OVERWEIGHT IN TEENAGERS IS INHERITED

It has been proved that our body build, especially our degree of fatness, is largely determined by our genes rather than our environment. This has been shown beyond doubt by observations of children who were adopted at birth and brought up by adoptive parents. It was found that these children, when they became young adults, had the body build, including the degree of fatness, of their natural parents (who had had no contact with them), and not that of their adoptive parents (who had fed them and brought them up).

Of course children can't become fat unless there is plenty of food, and family eating habits don't always help, but it is clear that there are 'fat' genes that we inherit, and these really determine how fat we can become. Everyone knows that obesity runs in families. If both parents are fat, there is an 80% chance that their child will be fat. If both parents are slim, it is likely that their child will be slim. Try fattening up a slim teenager who has slim parents, and you'll find it's virtually impossible: he or she will have hollow legs, and his or her capacity to eat will be enormous. Try thinning down a fat teenager who comes from a family with parents who are also fat, and you'll find it's just as difficult, unless he or she becomes ill.

SOME TEENAGERS BECOME OVERWEIGHT THROUGH INACTIVITY

We live in a society of cars and television. Both have a lot to answer for when it comes to the health of teenagers. If parents want their overweight teenager to get a bit slimmer, they should focus on increasing his or her physical activity. That isn't easy, but it is worth the effort just in improving wellbeing and fitness.

SOME ALTERATION TO EATING HABITS MAY BE HELPFUL, BUT DIETS ARE DEFINITELY OUT

Fat teenagers seldom benefit from diets, even though most have tried diets over and over again (without lasting success). Diets just set teenagers up for failure. Teenagers lose some weight during the first week or two, and everyone says: 'There. We know you can do it.' They can do it too, for a week or two. It is neither fair nor realistic, and certainly not healthy, to expect a teenager to live in a permanent state of starvation. Those who do so successfully may become stuck in a starvation mode of life, and tend to lose weight even when they are already desperately thin. This is the result of an eating disorder, anorexia nervosa. Fortunately very few teenagers go this far, but it is a risk for some strenuous dieters.

Parents will give the best help to their overweight teenager if they encourage exercise and combine it with advice on sensible eating, which includes:

- Don't skip breakfast or lunch. People who do this more than make up for it later in the day.

- Eat plenty of carbohydrates such as bread, cereals and fruit, rather than sugary snack foods.

- Avoid too much fat. (Don't remove fats altogether, however, as some fats in the meals are necessary for health.) Cut down on fried foods.

- Consider the type of fluids your teenager drinks. Fruit juices (even without added sugar) and regular soft drink have about 10% sugar, which can contribute quite a lot of calories.

- Make sure that all the family adopt healthy eating. It isn't fair for just one member to make changes.

- Watch out for saboteurs. Fathers may be a danger, also grandparents. They may feel that take-away snacks and soft drinks and sweets and cakes are everyone's right, and they like giving food to young people. It's a natural urge.

- Try to have some attractive low-energy snacks ready in the fridge for after school, when the urge to eat is almost irresistible.
- Allow a treat sometimes. It's something to look forward to.
- Don't make weight control a moral issue. The decision to control weight is the teenager's. If the teenager fails, at least they tried, and it's not a mortal sin.

FAT IS BEAUTIFUL

Who says that everyone has to be slim? Unfortunately, many of the magazines and fashions.

It may be much more helpful for the fat teenager to get good clothes, a good hairstyle, and attend to good personal grooming. Then they might find that they are just as beautiful and attractive as everyone else.

Dieting and eating disorders

THE DANGERS OF THE DIETING HABIT

Most teenage girls report trying to diet at least sometimes. Every now and again, someone is so successful at it that she can't break the dieting habit. She becomes thinner and thinner to the point that she endangers her health.

Dieting may become so entrenched that it is like an addiction that she couldn't give up even if she wanted to. But she doesn't want to. She has done so well in becoming slim, and it required so much will-power, that she doesn't want to stop and risk getting fat all over again. And she doesn't want anyone telling her that she should give up her very successful dieting and exercise program.

YOUNG PEOPLE TEND TO RECEIVE FALSE MESSAGES ABOUT WEIGHT

Perhaps as a result of current fashion which dictates that it is necessary to be slim to be attractive, perhaps as a result of the recurring theme in magazines for teenagers and women on how to lose weight in order to feel trim and terrific and to be more sexy, and perhaps because young people are so often urged to eat 'healthy' foods by organizations and some teachers and some dietitians (and everybody says that fats are 'unhealthy'), and perhaps for other reasons, some young people are at risk of developing eating disorders like anorexia nervosa and bulimia.

Boys can develop an eating disorder, but it is much commoner in girls and young women.

There are several sorts of eating disorders

Only a small proportion of young people develop anorexia nervosa. A larger number vomit after meals to control weight (usually as part of a cycle in which they first try to fast, then they binge eat, then they vomit). This is called bulimia nervosa.

There are several variants of these disorders, some not as dangerous as true anorexia, and less likely to become entrenched. Any teenager, however, who appears to be using severe and persistent methods to control weight is at risk.

HOW DO EATING DISORDERS DEVELOP? EARLY WARNING SIGNS

Eating disorders often develop gradually. At first it seems like sensible and healthy eating. The extra exercise seems excellent. Trimming off a bit of fat is applauded. Whether their daughter was fat before or not, parents seldom worry in the early stages of an eating disorder like anorexia. With progressive weight loss, parents may get anxious. Rightly so, because the dieting may become a habit, then an obsession. The danger then is that the longer the weight loss and anorexia have been present, and the longer the intervention is delayed, the worse the ultimate outlook as an adult.

Friends often worry that someone is dieting and losing weight before parents notice it. Girls are very good at disguising their thin body under loose clothing and modesty. They are fiercely proud of their ability to control their eating, and will resent anyone trying to stop them.

ANOREXIA NERVOSA, AND DOING SOMETHING ABOUT IT

If a teenager is clearly losing weight inappropriately and is becoming thin, if she is eating too little, or if the foods that she does eat are very low-energy foods, she should be told so by her family. She will probably resent this interference with her life, deny that she is dieting excessively, and vigorously maintain that she does not have a problem.

This makes it very difficult for her family. There will probably be tears and anger and promises to start eating and putting on weight. These are usually delaying tactics, and if parents are worried they should insist on a medical consultation at once. The sooner the better if she is to have the best outcome. If she is diagnosed as having anorexia nervosa she will need specialist help.

Sometimes the weight loss becomes so severe that the body can't provide enough energy from its reserves, and a number of things happen. Menstruation will stop. She will stop growing. Bones will lose some of their calcium and become weak. She may drive herself to continue exercising, but eventually even this cannot be maintained safely. She may become physically ill, feel cold, become faint, have low body temperature, slow heart rate, and low blood pressure.

At this stage, she will probably not be able to think rationally, and will not be able to make proper decisions for herself. If she

reaches this point she may need hospital care, and she certainly should not remain at school.

BULIMIA

Some teenagers make themselves vomit after meals in order to control their weight. They usually try to deceive their parents and others about what they are doing, and often are very successful in this. Often they manage to control their weight successfully by this means, even though they may eat large meals and sometimes indulge in quite gross snacking. They are often underweight, but may also be of normal weight.

Apart from the social disadvantages of this habit, there are some serious medical problems associated with it. These include loss of potassium from the body, with low levels in the blood, which may affect the heart. The habit may also damage tooth enamel through stomach acid juices in the vomit.

Most teenagers with bulimia are very preoccupied with their weight. They try fasting, but then get an overwhelming desire to eat (and overdo it). Then they feel bloated and anxious, and this is relieved only by vomiting. Sometimes they use laxatives to purge the bowel as well, but this does nothing for weight control.

There are effective treatments available for this disorder.

OTHER EATING DISORDERS

There are a number of disorders that may not be as serious as true anorexia nervosa, but which may nevertheless have serious consequences for a growing teenager.

One of these is quite common amongst female ballet dancers, gymnasts and athletes. The young person tries to lose weight and become slim to achieve better performance. She may be encouraged to do so by her coach. The trouble is that she may overdo it, become obsessive in her exercise program, and eat far less than she needs. She may take laxatives, diuretics or fibre pills in the mistaken belief that they will be effective in controlling weight. The outcome may include failure to grow properly and delayed puberty, or cessation of menstruation. She may eventually become less proficient in ballet or sport, as she will have lost muscle as well as fat.

Although some of these young people may develop true anorexia nervosa, and require specialist intervention, many do not have a severe psychological problem, and may be able to reverse their weight loss by simple counselling, dietary advice and limitations placed on their activity.

If a teenager does not respond promptly, the limitations may need to be severe and enforced. This will probably cause distress for the teenager, her coach and her parents, who may set great store on her performance. It will certainly require a cooperative plan that involves doctor, dietitian, coach, and parents as well as the teenager. In most cases the teenager will need to know that she cannot train or compete unless she has a certain agreed weight and eats adequately to maintain it.

CHAPTER 9

PHYSICAL HEALTH

Sleep: do they have enough?

'I can't get him to bed at night, and next morning he's impossible to get up. When I go to his room to wake him, he tells me to get lost. If I didn't keep on at him, he'd never get to school on time. If only he went to bed at a reasonable time, there'd be no problem.'

Peter's mother was sounding off about his general lack of organization, his bad moods and his frequent colds, all of which she attributed to lack of sleep.

Peter wasn't very impressed. 'Sure, Mum. If I went to bed early, I'd never get my homework done. And anyway I don't always go so late, except on weekends.'

'And Fridays, and when the football's on, and when there's a movie on telly you want to watch.'

This could have gone on for some time. Peter thought his mother was unreasonable, and his mother thought that he wasn't being sensible and wouldn't face facts. Considering that he was doing Year 10, and didn't always hand in school assignments on time, she probably had a point. Both were prepared to reconsider their

I'M DEFINITELY NOT TIRED!

*position if we could clarify how much
sleep he really needed and how he could
do all the things he wanted to do, and
his homework, in the available time.*

Getting teenagers to go to bed on time is a major battle for many parents. Even if they agree to stop watching television and go off to their rooms when parents ask them to, they often spend hours actually getting into bed, and then they listen to music on their headphones until they fall asleep, exhausted. Of course they are tired the next day. Naturally they would sleep in till midday in the holidays if parents let them.

Sleep requirements vary quite a lot between one child and another, and this is even more true during adolescence. Some studies have suggested that teenagers actually need more sleep than at other ages, perhaps because of teenagers' rapid growth and because they are often so very active during the day. Most will benefit from having at least 9 hours each night, and some will need 10 hours or even more. A few can cope with 8 hours, but any less will lead to a deficit which has to be made up, usually in weekends and holidays.

It seems likely that lack of sleep can lower teenagers' resistance to stress. This makes them more liable to colds and other minor infections. It also makes it harder to cope with the stress of daily living, with the pressures of school and the inevitable strains of family life.

HOW DO YOU TELL
IF YOUR TEENAGER IS HAVING
ENOUGH SLEEP?

Your teenager is probably not having enough sleep if they feel tired in the morning and find it very hard to get up. In weekends and holidays they may sleep late into the morning (not just an hour or so), and then wander round in an aimless fashion until something stirs them into action. All this suggests that the teenager has some sleep to catch up. The fact that they are full of energy late at night,

when any sensible human being would be thinking of bed, may mean that their time clock is out, in much the same way as someone who is jet-lagged.

Of course there are other explanations for late sleepers. Sometimes adolescents who are depressed or who have personal worries may find it hard to get to sleep, and then feel terrible in the morning. Altered sleep patterns may become a habit, and this can be awkward when a teenager returns to school after the holidays or when they start a job.

HOW DO YOU PERSUADE YOUR
TEENAGER TO GO TO BED?

By being very firm. By making rules for bed time that both parents are convinced are right, and which the teenager can agree to when it is discussed quietly and not just during a fight at midnight. The rules are governed by what parents think their teenager needs.

Fitting homework, school assignments, television, sport, fun, relaxation and social life into the short period between school and bedtime, to say nothing about meals and household chores, is a tricky business, and your teenager may need your help. Otherwise it is possible that they will do the things they enjoy first, and leave homework until they are too tired to do it or have to stay up late to finish it. It is possible that television will have to be restricted, and social life limited, during weekdays in school term.

*Immunization:
at teenage?*

We live in a society where most of the traditional and serious infectious diseases of childhood are now rare, and those that still exist are treatable or, like chicken pox, not usually serious.

Should we be worried about immunization for teenagers? They had their various shots for tetanus, diphtheria, whooping cough and poliomyelitis when they were younger. They probably had their measles immunization too. Parents aren't always sure what their teenage children have had, or when. Rubella immunization is important for girls, but now it is given to everyone. Tetanus booster shots are needed every 10 years throughout life. What about hepatitis?

Anyone who has experienced a community where most of the children are not immunized knows how devastating such diseases as measles or poliomyelitis or tuberculosis can be. The same is true for tetanus, the treatment for which can be very frightening. But very few parents have encountered these diseases, so they may not realize how important immunization has been in changing the nature of illness and death in our community.

MUMPS, MEASLES AND RUBELLA

These old diseases of childhood are still a risk if we do not maintain immunization. The effects of rubella (German measles) if it infects the unborn baby in early foetal life include heart abnormalities, deafness, visual defects, diabetes and sometimes mental problems.

It is recommended that all children should have booster immunizations for these diseases in early puberty. A combined vaccine, MMR, is freely available.

HEPATITIS B

Hepatitis B infection is usually spread in Australia through sharing intravenous drug needles, and through sexual contact. It is potentially a very serious disease, and may cause liver damage and failure.

The risk of this infection, and the carrier rate of the virus, varies greatly throughout the world and in various community groups in Australia and New Zealand. It is certainly present amongst young people in Australia and New Zealand, and is even more prevalent in some countries in South East Asia. The infection is more easily acquired than AIDS, as the virus seems to survive outside the human body for long periods. It can be transmitted through blood, semen, vaginal secretions and saliva.

There are increasing reports of the disease being acquired in heterosexual contacts when one of the partners has had previous contact with the virus. It is likely that apart from sexual and needle spread, the virus can be passed from one person to another through casual contacts in sport or in the playground, if there has been bleeding from an injury. This is why there are strict rules for treating sporting injuries, and for not sharing towels or other personal items after sport.

The answer is for all teenagers to become immunized. This is common practice now, not just for teenagers at risk. It will probably become universal practice eventually.

HEPATITIS A

The risk of hepatitis A is not high in Australia at present. There is, however, a risk for those travelling overseas to some countries where the prevalence is high. Then immunization is a wise precaution.

Hygiene: a running battle

'I wish you'd talk to him about personal hygiene, doctor. He hardly ever showers, I don't know how often he changes his socks. His room smells, but he won't let me in to clean it, and he won't do anything himself.'

Alan's rolling eyes and reproachful glances at his mother told me that a discussion on washing himself and cleaning his room would not be his idea of a useful encounter with his doctor. In fact, in Alan's opinion — if anyone asked him, which he thought was most unlikely — the whole consultation was doomed to be a waste of his time.

Another mother, whose son was extremely conscious of cleanliness, said that one reason he went to bed so late was that he had to spend half an hour just washing and looking at himself in the mirror when he was undressing. Her son looked at her and said: (a) she was lying, and (b) it was something she didn't need to go round telling everybody.

SOME TEENAGERS SPEND HOURS IN THE SHOWER

They use up all the hot water, keep everyone waiting for the bathroom, and then cheerfully emerge all clean and shining as if they had only been five minutes. Girls (and some boys) will shampoo their hair just about every day. It takes them hours, it is absolutely essential, if they missed doing it just once their hair would be a mess and they couldn't consider going out with their friends.

What do teenagers do in the shower for so long? Apart from the nice, warm, relaxing feel of running hot water, most teenagers like to admire (and criticize) their body as it

COURTESY OF 'FLYCAM'

develops. The shower gives them the opportunity to do so in private, with no-one speculating on what they might be doing. They aren't actually doing much at all, just relaxing and soaping and enjoying and being private. And they like their bodies to be clean and attractive, not for the benefit of their family, of course, but for themselves and for other teenagers. Or course, some use the shower to wake themselves up in the morning, just like adults.

If you or the rest of the family think your teenager is hogging too much of the hot water, or making everyone late by spending hours in the bathroom, have a family conference and make rules for everybody, including the recalcitrant teenager. You may have to get one of those kitchen timers to sound an alarm after the agreed time, because 5 or 10 minutes pass very quickly when you are relaxing in the shower. But at least be pleased that your teenager is taking pride in their personal appearance and is keeping clean.

OTHER TEENAGERS NEGLECT HYGIENE

What about teenagers who neglect personal hygiene? At their age you can't throw them into the bath as you could when they were children. Telling teenagers that they smell just makes them angry. Hinting that their acne is due to being dirty isn't fair (or true).

Does it matter?

Firstly: does it really matter if teenagers are a bit dirty or don't take a shower every day? Who is suffering?

If they aren't worried by it, and they don't have a rash or skin disease, and they don't smell too bad, then it might be better to leave them to sort it out for themselves, rather than make an issue of something that will probably only make them and their parents angry. In time, maybe they will meet someone they want to impress, and then they'll change.

If they really do smell horrible, and it's not just adolescent smell (which they can't help),

perhaps they have foot tinea which may need treatment. If they have poor genital hygiene, this will need some discussion with them.

If it's their clothes that smell, perhaps they will at least let you wash them, even if you can't wash the wearers.

Poor hygiene can be a sign of depression

Perhaps personal hygiene really does matter, not in itself, but because it is a sign that all is not well for your teenager. Sometimes, if teenagers are very unhappy or depressed, they will neglect their personal appearance and grooming and not care if they are dirty.

Are you missing other signs of depression in your teenager, such as sleep disturbance (they can't get to sleep, then feel awful in the morning), isolating themselves from the family, feeling low, crying a lot, giving up friends, or dropping sport?

Could your teenager be using drugs? One of the signs can be loss of interest in personal appearance and hygiene.

If the only problem for your teenager is poor hygiene, and you feel comfortable about discussing it with them, talk about the personal satisfaction of feeling good about oneself, keeping one's body in good shape, and looking nice.

Genital hygiene

Boys may have some trouble keeping their genital area clean. They would probably be better off wearing boxer shorts, which are loose fitting and where there is ventilation, than tight jockey shorts or briefs. If a boy has not been circumcised, he may develop problems of hygiene under the foreskin, unless he retracts it under the shower regularly and cleans underneath. If he can't retract his foreskin, it may be wise for him to consult his doctor about it, particularly if it is becoming inflamed.

Girls may develop difficulties in genital hygiene. They should have been shown, as children, how to wipe themselves after a bowel action, so germs from the back passage don't pass forwards. They may need some advice when they start menstruating. If there is a persistent discharge, then it would be wise for her to see her doctor.

DENTAL HYGIENE

Most Australian children are lucky, as fluoride deficiency in water has been largely corrected. As a result, teenagers tend to have healthy teeth, in marked contrast to teenagers growing up 50 years ago, or to youth in many other countries. In America, for instance, dental health is a major health issue for youth, as so many have dental decay. Even in Australia, teenagers sometimes need to be reminded that their teeth are both important and vulnerable.

Menstruation

IRREGULAR PERIODS

It is usual for periods to be irregular for the first year or two. They tend to be quite naturally irregular, but will be even more so if the girl is under stress, is dieting excessively, or exercising very vigorously. Sooner or later they become regular.

PADS OR TAMPONS?

A girl can use a pad or a tampon, whichever suits her. It used to be thought that a girl who was a virgin might have difficulty with a tampon, as it was thought it could damage the entry to the vagina. This is rarely so, and even a girl who has never had intercourse can usually use a tampon, though she might need to discuss this with her mother — the size and brand of tampon, how to insert it, whether to use KY jelly and, most important of all, to change it frequently and regularly. For most girls, however, it is probably sensible to start with a pad.

PERIOD PAIN

Once ovulation has started, some girls have painful cramps during their period.

This is often quite well controlled by Panadol or aspirin, provided it is taken as soon as the pain starts. If the pain is severe, there are other medications which are usually effective in controlling the pain, and it is worth consulting a doctor about this.

There is usually no reason why a girl should not do sport during her period. It depends on how she feels, and whether she has bad period pain.

Acne: zapping the zit

Most teenagers get at least some acne. Boys are more liable to get it, and to get it worse. Only a few teenagers get really severe and persisting acne, and for them it can be a real misery. It can spoil much of their social life and damage their self-esteem. The most severe form of acne can leave scars.

Not all parents take acne seriously. These parents know that they survived it in their youth. They don't think that their teenager looks so bad, it's just part of growing up. They may think that it is partly the teenager's own fault: if he didn't eat so much junk food, if he washed his face sometimes and didn't put that stuff on his hair, if she got a bit more sleep, if she ate her green vegetables and had more fruit . . .

SNIGGER!

ACNE IS NOT CAUSED BY BAD DIET OR POOR HYGIENE

It is most unlikely that fatty foods or lack of cleanliness have anything to do with acne at all. Some teenagers, however, do feel that chocolate brings out new pimples. One boy I knew was convinced that chillies, his favourite food and a common ingredient in his family cooking, gave him acne. It is also possible that some things like stress and lack of sleep may make acne worse in some teenagers.

Acne is due to the effect of the hormones that are so active during puberty, so it is certainly not the teenager's fault. These hormones are known as androgens. (Androgens are the hormones that tend to produce male characteristics. The main one is called testosterone. Even girls make some androgens.)

Androgens are the key to the cause of acne, but that doesn't explain why some teenagers get severe acne, while others, who have just as much hormone circulating about, don't seem to get it at all. Most unfair. There is certainly a genetic factor: a boy who has severe acne often finds that his father had the same problem as a teenager. It is all to do with the way the oil glands in the skin react to the androgens.

HOW DOES ACNE DEVELOP?

At puberty, the body produces increasing amounts of these androgens. While these hormones lead to some of the changes of puberty, they are also having an effect on the oil glands in the skin. These glands are called sebaceous glands, and most of them are in the skin of the face, back and chest. The sebaceous glands make an oily substance called sebum, and this sebum makes the skin smooth and moist.

Sometimes the sebaceous glands overreact to the androgens. Then they may

FACTS ABOUT ACNE

1. There is little point in making drastic changes in diet

There is no evidence that diet plays any part in treatment of acne, but if a teenager finds that chocolate or some other food seems to make the acne worse, then it is sensible to try avoiding those foods.

2. Acne is not due to poor hygiene

It is good to keep clean, and to wash the face and neck with a mild soap. While washing, be careful not to be too rough, as this may damage the skin still more. There is no need to use an antiseptic soap.

3. Acne is made worse by squeezing and squashing

However irritating and embarrassing the acne is, touching and scratching it won't help.

4. Exposure to the open air and to sea-water helps

Excessive exposure to sun is, of course, dangerous. Some creams and lotions make the skin very sensitive to sunlight, so be warned. Use sunscreen by all means, but it may be better to use an alcohol-based one rather than a cream.

5. Avoid ointments and greasy preparations

These usually make the acne worse. Most acne is in rather oily skin anyway. Some lotions tend to dry the skin, and this is preferable.

6. Some cosmetics can make acne worse

This is true particularly if they are used too much. Some drugs, too. Be careful.

7. A healthy lifestyle is best

A healthy lifestyle, with plenty of sleep, exercise, relaxing leisure, and the ability to cope effectively with stress, is good for everyone.

make too much sebum, and to make matters worse, the tubes from the glands tend to block up, so the sebum can't escape onto the surface of the skin. When this happens a blackhead develops. This is sometimes called a comedo. The black colour is not dirt: it is the colour that develops when sebum comes in contact with air.

If certain bacterial germs get into the blackhead, they break down the fatty sebum into substances which cause skin irritation. This leads to inflammation, and that's when the pimple starts. First with redness and swelling, then later pus develops. This is very embarrassing for a teenager, who will probably squash the pimple to squeeze out the pus. This tends to make the skin even more inflamed.

CREAMS AND LOTIONS: WHICH ONES, AND HOW DO THEY WORK?

There's no perfect treatment, and only time cures acne. There are many good treatments to control it, however, and the best one for a

particular teenager depends on the severity of the acne, whether there is inflammation, and some other factors. Sometimes a doctor will suggest one treatment before trying another, and sometimes a skin specialist may be needed.

Damage control

There really isn't much you can do once a pimple has developed, except to cover it up with a cosmetic. It is helpful to dry it out, and some alcohol preparations can be tried. If you do use a cosmetic to cover it up, use a drying one, such as a lotion or cream, not an ointment.

Prevention of new acne

This is the best way to treat acne, and leads to much better results. The trouble is that you may have to wait some weeks, maybe 6 to 8, for the treatment to show full benefit, and some creams can actually make it a bit worse before it gets better. Teenagers tend to get discouraged long before 6 weeks have gone by, and they may think the treatment was a waste of time, and give up before it has had a chance to work.

For prevention treatment, it's no good just dabbing the cream or lotion on the pimples: they are a bit of a lost cause. It should be put on all the area where new acne may develop, and that usually means the whole face. But keep it away from the eyes. It is also usually important to apply it when the skin is thoroughly dry: say half an hour after washing.

There are several preparations that are effective. They work in various ways. They may reduce the amount of the sebum produced by the glands. They also tend to unblock the gland openings and reduce the thick outer layer of skin so that the sebum can escape more easily. They may also fight the germs that cause inflammation. The common ones are benzoyl-peroxide in an alcohol- or water-based preparation, and retinoic acid in a cream or lotion. They work in slightly different ways, and it is important to use them in the right way. The teenager should discuss this with the doctor or pharmacist.

Some of the creams are rather expensive, so if large areas of the skin are affected, like the back or chest, there are cheaper and quite effective preparations available. Examples are salicylic acid in alcohol (2 to 10%), and sulphur precipitate in calamine lotion (5 to 15%). They can be applied to a large area overnight.

What about antibiotics?

For more severe acne, especially if there are pustules, it is often helpful to use an antibiotic, sometimes as a cream but more usually as a pill or capsule. The course of oral antibiotics needs to go for at least 3, and usually 6 months to be effective.

Other treatments?

There are other treatments, some for very severe acne that might cause scarring, some for the acne that is particularly severe during menstruation. Some of these should be prescribed by a specialist, and all need detailed instructions on how to use them safely.

Almost all acne can be helped by proper treatment. There are a number of new treatments and nobody should have to go through teenage with severe and embarrassing acne.

Teenage illnesses

TEENAGERS ARE MOSTLY HEALTHY

Teenagers are usually pretty healthy, at least from a physical viewpoint, and they need to see a doctor less often than at almost any other time of life. But they do get ill sometimes. The most common things that take a teenager to a doctor are respiratory infections, minor injuries, severe headaches, abdominal pains (could it be appendicitis?) and fever. Skin problems, such as acne, warts and moles, are a regular annoyance for teenagers, though they often don't consult their doctor about them.

CHRONIC ILLNESS OR DISABILITY

It has been estimated in a major survey in North America, that up to 30% of teenagers have some form of chronic illness or disability. Many of these are fairly minor (such as nasal allergies), some may not be too much of a problem for the teenager (such as the need to wear glasses), but many are a significant influence in teenagers' lives, particularly at a time when they are often desperate to be 'normal'. One thing the survey showed was that as far as freedom from chronic illness or disability is concerned, only 70% of teenagers are so fortunate.

Asthma

The commonest chronic condition in adolescence is asthma. If we include all those who just get wheezing with exercise, or in cold weather, as well as those who get quite severe attacks of asthma, 20% of teenagers have asthma. Even teenagers who have had only mild symptoms during childhood may get a severe attack when they are older, particularly during adolescence. A Victorian survey showed that the old belief that children grow out of asthma is just not true. Or at least not for significant asthma. Of course some with mild symptoms may have no further trouble, while others may develop asthma for the first time during their teenage years.

All this emphasizes that teenagers who have asthma should keep in touch with their doctor and make sure that they are getting the best treatment. They may need treatment for attacks and may need to carry an inhaler around with them at all times. Some will need treatment to take each day to prevent further attacks of wheeze.

SOME MEDICAL CONDITIONS START IN ADOLESCENCE

Some medical conditions often start in adolescence, or occur most often then.

Glandular fever

This occurs most often in adolescence. It often starts with a fever and sore throat. It's infectious, it tends to hang around, and can be quite severe. Glandular fever is often thought of as an adolescent disease. It was once called 'the kissing disease' because this is how it often spread — quite embarrassing for a young teenager in the past.

Migraine

Migraine is another condition that can start in adolescence. Often one or other parent also gets migraine, so they tend to know what is happening, but there is always the worry that it may be something more serious. There are treatments that can make migraine much less of a problem than it once was.

Epilepsy

Some forms of epilepsy start in adolescence. The first time a child or teenager has some type of fit or turn, it is very frightening for their parents, and alarming enough for the child or teenager. Fits or turns very seldom signal something serious going on inside the head (such as a brain tumour), but they obviously need to be investigated by a doctor. Some forms of epilepsy can be brought on by lack of sleep, or stress, or drugs. Most forms of epilepsy are readily controlled by medication. Some teenagers may have just one fit, and never any more.

Diabetes

Diabetes can occur at any time during childhood or later life, but the form that requires insulin treatment tends to come on early in life, particularly during adolescence. Most people are well aware of the warning signs (excessive thirst, excessive urine and weight loss) that almost always precede the diagnosis of diabetes. The warning signs in teenagers can be confusing: teenagers often drink a lot anyway, they tend not to tell their parents about their urine habits, and they are often quite pleased to be losing weight. Any teenager who has these signs — drinking a lot, getting up at night to pass urine, or who is losing weight without any other obvious reason — should be checked for diabetes by his or her doctor.

CARING FOR A CHRONIC ILLNESS CAN CAUSE PROBLEMS

Chronic illness may present special problems for teenagers and the parents. On the one hand, teenagers may need their parents to help in their care. On the other hand, like all adolescents, they have to develop self-reliance and independence. This may be impaired if their parents tend to watch them and advise them all the time.

They may need to be taken to the doctor (even if it's only to provide transport or give moral support). They may need looking after during an attack of asthma, or if diabetes gets out of control. They may need reminding about their medication and other treatment. Some studies have shown that many teenagers can be hopeless at remembering to take medication regularly. They forget. They feel that it isn't necessary if they are feeling well (even though the medication is aimed to keep them feeling well and to prevent them getting sick). They don't like being reminded that they have a medical condition that requires medication.

The problem of supervision

'Every time that I have my epilepsy tablets I say to myself: "I'm an epileptic." I hate that, so sometimes I just don't take my tablets, so I feel I don't have epilepsy that day. It's stupid, I know, but it's worth it just to be normal for a few days.'

This was said to me by a boy who had had an epileptic fit when he was having a bath. He had nearly drowned, and his parents were angry with him because he hadn't been taking his tablets.

It's no wonder that many parents feel that they have to watch and supervise their teenager who has a chronic condition needing treatment. But there are problems in doing this.

There is the risk that the teenager will have difficulty in ever taking responsibility for his or her own care. If you never make mistakes because your mother protects you from doing so, you may make a mess of things when you eventually leave home as an adult and can't rely on her. Worse still, you might have trouble in leaving home at all.

Too much supervision in one aspect of a teenager's life (their health care) might intrude into their social life or personal development. It might make it difficult to do all the teenage things that are exciting and fun and maybe just a bit risky, but worth it when it is part of belonging to a group. Things that a parent mightn't approve of, especially if they were constantly worrying about their teenager's medical condition.

How much should parents do for their teenagers, how much can they trust their teenagers to look after themselves? How should they remind their teenagers about taking medication, how much should parents bite their tongues, knowing that their teenagers really need parental nagging, even though teenagers hate it? How much to let them run the risk of illness, how much to intervene to prevent it?

These are all decisions that must be made according to how mature and reliable your teenager is, and how serious the illness. Talk it over with your teenager. 'How can I help you?' 'Would you like me to remind you to take your tablets at night?' 'Shall I put them out with your breakfast things?' 'Shall we give you a go at looking after yourself quite independently for a while, and if it doesn't work out, then you can decide what help you would like?'

A delicate balance: supervision and protection

It's a delicate balance between protecting your child, whom you have nurtured all these years, and letting your child develop self-reliance as he or she grows up.

The overriding factor is whether the consequences of the illness could be life threatening. If not, let your teenager make mistakes. Give your teenager the credit of trying. Give him or her a second chance. Talk it over with your teenager. Perhaps talk it over with the teenager and his or her doctor, together.

SOMETIMES IT'S HARD TO LET GO

Sometimes it's very difficult for parents to let go, to relinquish care after being so very responsible throughout their child's early life. Perhaps it might be helpful to talk this over with your teenager's doctor, so you can be sure that all your early care has set the groundwork for his or her future development.

Seeing a doctor: a confidential encounter

Some time ago a number of young people in their late teens were discussing their experiences when they went to see a doctor. They had come together because they had had some problems, and because they had been asked to give their views about medical consultations.

'I went to see our family doctor because I was having sex with my boyfriend, and I wanted to go on the pill. I didn't want my parents to know. They couldn't cope. The doctor told me I was only 15 and he had to tell my parents. I said no, but he did anyway. I couldn't trust him after that.'

'I go to see a doctor about my kidney condition. She tells me what I have to do. I can't understand half of what she says, but my Mum likes her.'

'My mother insists on going to the doctor with me. It's embarrassing. She answers half the questions he asks me.

Sometimes I don't get a say at all. She says that I wouldn't tell him everything if I went by myself. I certainly wouldn't say all the things she does. How would she know how I feel?'

'My mum says: "Do you want me to come in with you, dear?" If I say no it would hurt her feelings. I tried it once, and she said: "Oh well if you don't want me any more," and went really quiet, as if I'd insulted her. Now she just sits there, but I can't ask all the questions I'd like. Some would upset her. And I'd feel too embarrassed.'

'My parents go: "What did you say to the doctor? And what did she say to you?" And when I say: "Just about my periods," Mum goes: "Why didn't you tell her about your headaches? We can't trust you to go by yourself."'

Some of the teenagers said that they really liked their GP, and felt very comfortable going to him or her. Others felt that they would really prefer a doctor of their own, and not someone who might easily tell their parents about them. They all felt that privacy and confidentiality were very important. Sometimes there were things that they wanted to talk to someone about, like smoking or drugs or sexual feelings or feeling depressed, things that they just didn't feel that their parents could handle.

Mothers get used to taking their children to the doctor and telling the doctor about their children's problems. Some mothers may just naturally go on doing so long after their children have become adolescent, when they could perfectly well do the talking themselves, and answer the doctor's questions, and understand what they were supposed to do.

This is quite understandable. After all, mothers are still responsible for their teenagers, and they still look after them when they are sick. They still worry about them. And they never know how far they can trust their teenager to tell the doctor about all the symptoms and problems. And then to get instructions about the treatment right.

WHEN SHOULD A TEENAGER BE ENCOURAGED TO SEE HIS OR HER DOCTOR ALONE?

The answer is: as soon as a teenager feels that he or she would like to. It depends on how mature the teenager is. There is a legal concept of the 'mature minor' which suggests that teenagers who are under legal age — 18 in most states, but 16 is normally regarded as competent to make decisions — (and therefore called minors), could be responsible to make decisions about their treatment without their parents. They could

do this if they were mature enough to give a reasonably accurate account of their problem, and if they could understand the explanation given by the doctor. They should be able to understand the nature of the treatment and the way it would help, and could be expected to carry the treatment out reliably.

That may be asking a bit much of some teenagers, even some adults. It is, however, quite a helpful concept, and one which doctors must decide for themselves, before they prescribe for a teenager who is under the age of 16 and living at home. The legal aspects of this vary from state to state and certainly may be different from what parents may expect if they came from another country. The underlying principle, however, is to provide the best treatment for the teenager, and to respect the teenager's confidence.

Some parents may be dismayed to think that their daughter, aged 16 and living with them, could go to a doctor and demand that the doctor doesn't tell her parents what she came for and what the treatment was. However, some teenagers would be dismayed if they felt that a doctor had to tell their parents about the reasons why they came to see him or her.

Of course, this situation doesn't arise very often. Teenagers usually want their parents at least to drive them to the doctor, even if they don't go into the room with them, so it is rare for parents not to know what the problem is. Certainly, if there is any question of a threat to life (such as risk of suicide, or a very dangerous illness needing parental involvement), the doctor must tell the parents, but will always tell the teenager that they are going to do so.

The following is a reasonable guide to when teenagers should be encouraged to see their doctor alone:

- When they are 14: only if they want to.
- When they are 15: some of the time.
- When they are 16: most of the time.
- When they are 17: all of the time.

There will always be exceptions and special circumstances. Sometimes a male doctor will prefer a girl's mother to be in the room during an examination, rather than a nurse whom the girl doesn't know. Sometimes a teenager will deny that she has a problem (such as anorexia), when the parents know that she has. Then it will be essential that parents go in with the teenager, at least at first.

Sometimes a 14-year-old boy will not want his mother to be present during a physical examination. Or a girl may not want her father to be present during the examination. Parents need to be sensitive about this. A teenage boy, for example, may not like to ask his parents to leave him with the doctor. If the boy does ask, his parents will probably assume that he is going to tell the doctor something awful about them. Actually he is much more likely to want to talk about his puberty development or how he is teased about being short, or something very embarrassing like that.

Even more important for teenagers, however, is to have a chance to talk about issues like drugs and smoking and alcohol and sexually transmitted diseases and contraception without parents being present.

PRIVACY AND CONFIDENTIALITY

Teenagers value their privacy very highly. They resent it if parents or other adults talk about their private problems with anyone else. This is particularly so in their relationship with their doctor. If teenagers trust their doctor, they will probably tell him or her very personal things that they may be anxious about, but which they don't want to worry their parents with. If their doctor feels strongly that they should discuss this with their parents, the doctor will try to persuade them to do so. If they refuse, then the doctor must respect their desire for confidentiality.

Unless a doctor thought there was a risk of death, he or she mustn't break this confidentiality. It wouldn't be ethical and it would probably destroy a teenager's trust. A teenager's trust in their doctor is a very precious thing in their relationship. A doctor is privileged to have a teenager's trust; without it, a doctor will have difficulty in helping a teenager with any of their health problems. Helping might mean simple things, like taking antibiotics on schedule. It is even more vital in the complex care of chronic disease, or when there are psychological or behavioural difficulties.

WHAT IF PARENTS FEEL IT IS ESSENTIAL TO TALK TO THEIR TEENAGER'S DOCTOR ABOUT THEIR TEENAGER, EVEN IF THEIR TEENAGER DOESN'T WANT THEM TO?

If parents are sufficiently worried about their teenager, they should tell them that they wish to talk to their doctor. They should ask the teenager to be present, so they aren't talking behind their back. Even if they are going to say things that will upset their teenager, it probably won't be anything that hasn't come out many times at home. They shouldn't see their teenager's doctor without warning them first.

The real difficulty is for the doctor to talk to parents without first discussing this with their patient, the teenager. The doctor will want to ask the teenager's permission first. I usually find that teenagers give that permission readily enough, but they may stipulate certain things that must not be revealed (such as marijuana use, or sexual activity). Parents respect that, so long as everyone is open about things that really matter.

WHAT IF PARENTS REALLY NEED TO SUPERVISE TREATMENT?

If parents are worried about the extent to which their teenager is following instructions or carrying out treatment, they may need to step in and supervise. They will need to know all the details of treatment. They should warn their teenager that they feel they must help, and that they need to discuss with their teenager's doctor how best to do it. If there is resistance, have the discussion together with the doctor, who may be in a better position to negotiate a deal which allows parents to make sure that the treatment is followed.

WHEN SHOULD TEENAGERS HAVE THEIR OWN MEDICARE CARD?

As soon as they ask for it. When parents feel that they can trust their teenager to go to their doctor alone, and certainly by the age of 16 or 17. Having a Medicare card gives teenagers a sense of responsibility, and demonstrates that their parents trust them. It lets them see a doctor of their own choice when they feel more comfortable to do so.

CHAPTER 10

Drugs, Cigarettes, Alcohol

Experimenting with drugs

Most teenagers like to try out new experiences. That's part of growing up, and it is as natural as the way toddlers like to explore their world. And just as risky. In early adolescence, teenagers like to experiment and are easily influenced by other teenagers to do things that they know their parents wouldn't approve of. This is a dilemma for them, because they don't want to disobey their parents, but it's not cool to do what parents tell you to do all of the time. Doing things that your parents wouldn't like helps make you part of a teenage group, and for some teenagers, this is very important indeed.

If there are problems in the life of a teenager, perhaps family problems, perhaps school difficulties, perhaps difficulties in making friends, then being part of a group that does things like trying drugs may be one way of compensating for all the bad things they see in their lives.

Alcohol and nicotine are the most common drugs that teenagers use. Later in adolescence, marijuana becomes common. Some young teenagers try sniffing various volatile substances like petrol, aerosols and glue. Some older teenagers try almost anything they can find in their family medicine cupboard, like sleeping tablets, hay-fever tablets and tranquillizers. They often try a cocktail of drugs including alcohol, so they can experience the combined effects of a potentially dangerous mixture. Older adolescents may try amphetamine.

Any teenager who is acting strangely and out of character, or who is excessively drowsy, might have taken a drug. Or been given one. If there is a concern for health or even survival, it is possible to check if they have had a drug by urine screening tests available at major hospitals.

The transition to narcotics is fortunately uncommon in teenagers in our society, but a very real risk for some, particularly if they have left home and are living on the street.

SNIFFING, AMPHETAMINES AND BENZODIAZEPINES

Inhalants

Almost all materials teenagers may use to sniff or inhale are solvents. Solvents include glues, petrol, spray paints and some aerosols. They depress brain function, but people who try inhaling solvents get a feeling of intoxication and of wellbeing. They may become dizzy and feel they are floating. They tend to have impaired judgment, and in rebreathing the solvent in a bag, may run the risk of asphyxiation. This is dangerous, and apart from the risk of damaging the body (the brain and the liver), there have been deaths from inhaling solvents. Chrome paint spray (chroming) is particularly dangerous.

Amphetamines

Amphetamine is a synthetic stimulant of the brain. It has been used in the past as a medical drug to curb appetite. The common name for it is speed, but it has had many other names. It comes as a tablet, but some drug users dissolve it in water and inject it.

Amphetamine gives a feeling of elation. It often makes people talkative, restless and wakeful and have unusual volatile behaviour. Excessive use can cause confusion, sleeplessness, hallucinations and paranoid thinking. Users have dilated pupils, little appetite and a rapid heart rate. There is always the risk of overdose, and the bad effects of mixing with a variety of drugs.

Benzodiazepines

These are commonly prescribed as tranquillizers and sedatives, and include drugs like Valium and Serepax and Rohypnol. Many households have some in their medicine cabinet, and many parents and grandparents have supplies close to their bed. If there are any in the house, a teenager will find them if he or she really wants to.

Benzodiazepines may have a calming, euphoric and sleepy effect. Their misuse may lead to incoordination, delirium and nightmares.

The great majority of teenagers never use these drugs. All the same, parents should know what drugs there are in the medicine cabinet, and throw out those that aren't being used, particularly if they might be attractive to a teenager.

Drugs: are they using them?

Paul's mother had brought him along because he was consistently late for school or didn't get there at all. Sometimes he set off to go, but met up with friends and missed classes for the day. His parents found it increasingly hard to talk to him, and he was becoming moody and withdrawn. He had given up most of his old friends, had acquired some undesirable new ones, and had dropped out of sport.

He had stolen money from his mother and possibly other members of the family. He seemed to be neglecting his personal hygiene, and his room was a mess.

The school counsellor thought he was depressed, as indeed he was, and wasn't sufficiently 'goal-orientated'. His father thought he had an attitude problem, and needed to develop better motivation towards his schoolwork.

When Paul discussed this after his parents had left the room, he freely admitted he was using drugs almost every day. School was of little interest to him, and he often arrived stoned on marijuana. He had to spend quite a lot of his time and effort working out how to get money to pay for his drugs.

When he eventually agreed to tell his parents about this, they were devastated. It had never occurred to them that he could be on drugs, but when they thought about it, it seemed to explain everything, except why he started using drugs in the first place.

Most parents have a pretty good idea whether their teenager smokes cigarettes. Alcohol is harder to be sure about; after all, most teenagers do drink occasionally, and they may seem a bit high after parties. The real worry for parents is whether their teenagers are using other drugs, particularly marijuana, but also drugs like amphetamines and narcotics. How can parents tell if their teenager is using these drugs? If parents were to ask their teenager, it would mean that they don't trust them, and then that may make things worse. And if parents do ask, and their teenager denies it, how can parents be sure they are not lying?

DANGER SIGNS

There are a number of danger signs that should alert parents that their teenager could be using drugs. None of these signs alone may have much significance, but taken as a group, they should raise suspicion. Watch for the following signs in your teenager:

- Has difficulty in engaging in any serious conversation. Refuses to discuss things, and discipline just makes them angry.

- Friends or teachers are worried that your teenager's personality seems to have changed.

- Shows little concern for what their behaviour might be doing to other members of the family. They blame other members of the family for fights and arguments.

- Drops old friends and hangs out with teenagers who are often older and who have dropped out of school or got into trouble.

- Gets unexplained phone calls at odd hours, and visits by strange youths who drop in unexpectedly and don't get introduced.

- Appears depressed, and has concerns that the future holds nothing for them. 'Might as well die. Wouldn't worry me.'

- Constantly needs money. Unexplained loss of money by other members of the family or visitors. Quite large amounts may be involved.

- Lies about school attendance, or where they have been. Goes out a lot and refuses to say where. Seems to use the family home just for sleep and occasional food.

- Has become violent towards siblings or parents, often without provocation. If they are hurt or upset, the teenager says: 'They deserved it.'

- Inappropriate sexual behaviour. May be worried that she could be pregnant.

- Shows mood swings. Often depressed, but at other times euphoric. Sometimes seems dazed, unconcerned about anything. Outbursts of anger.

- Fails at school, with poor grades and bad reports, out of keeping with past performance.
- Has difficulty in sleeping at night, but may drop off to sleep at odd times during the day.

If a number of these signs are noticed, parents should at least consider that their teenage son or daughter may be using drugs on a regular basis. Whether a parent should confront their teenager, or take them to the family doctor, or ask a respected member of the family to discuss it with their teenager, will depend on how things stand between yourself and your teenager, but the worst thing is to do nothing and ignore the problem.

Teenagers may become quite dependent on drugs, and can be desperate to obtain them. They may neglect themselves, their schoolwork and their family as they become preoccupied with obtaining the drug and seeking the relief or pleasure that the drug affords. The longer the habit persists, the more entrenched the dependence and the harder it is for parents to do anything to help their teenager.

For all of these reasons, parents who suspect that their teenager is involved with drugs should do something about it as soon as they can.

Smoking: tell him to stop, doctor

'He's started smoking, doctor. I wish you'd tell him about what will happen to him. We've tried, but he doesn't pay any notice.'

'Everyone smokes, Mum. I don't smoke that much anyway. Why don't you tell Dad to stop, he's more likely to die from lung cancer than I am.'

There have been many surveys of when people start smoking. All agree that most people started smoking when they were teenagers. A survey of Victorian students, carried out in 1992, showed that 5.1% of Year 7 students smoked regularly. The proportion increases steadily, so that 20.8% of Year 10 students, and 23.7% of Year 11 students, smoke regularly. The numbers increase as they get into their twenties, so that most school leavers who smoke regularly continue to do so into adult life.

It was also found that by Year 9, girls were more likely to smoke than boys. Other surveys confirm this trend, and also suggest that girls tend to smoke, on average, more heavily than boys.

Teenagers are more likely to take up smoking if one or other parent, or an older sibling, smokes. They are more likely to smoke if they belong to a group of friends who smoke. It probably helps bond the group, and gives them an opportunity to share (cigarettes are a good entry to a group,

and may help to open a conversation and make friends). They are more likely to smoke if they lack self-esteem and don't feel good about themselves. Teenagers who come from families who have split up, or have single parents, are at greater risk of taking up smoking.

As any heavy smoker who has tried to give up smoking knows, cigarettes are very addictive. It has been said that nicotine is as addictive as heroin: giving up may not be quite so physically painful, but the need to have a cigarette while trying to stop smoking may be very strong indeed, and the desire to resume after quitting can be too much for many adults, let alone for teenagers.

It's even harder to stop if some of your friends smoke in your presence. You're bound to fail if you aren't convinced that you really want to stop anyway.

If it's that bad, why do so many young teenagers start smoking? They know that their parents don't want them to. They have certainly been told over and over again that it is bad for their health, and lung cancer is a rather horrible way to die. They may have asthma, or a friend may, and that doesn't necessarily put them off. It's expensive. They are liable to get punished if they get caught smoking at school or at home. It's against the law to supply tobacco to a minor, so it should be hard to get cigarettes (but it isn't).

What's so good about smoking, then? It's natural to experiment, so it's understandable to try just one or two cigarettes, and that doesn't make you addicted. It's an adult thing to do. It's cool. It's sharing with friends. It's a way into a group. It's something to do if you are at a party, and you don't know too many people. It stops you looking awkward, you have something to do with your hands. It's enjoyable. It relaxes you and makes you feel good. It stops you getting bored. Lots of people you admire smoke, so it helps you identify with them.

With all these advantages, it's a wonder that more teenagers don't smoke. The fact is that most don't really want to. They can think of better ways of spending their money. They like feeling healthy. They want to keep fit. Kissing is better if neither of you smoke. Smoking's stupid.

HOW DO YOU PREVENT YOUR TEENAGER FROM SMOKING?

You may not be able to, but you can try.

- Don't smoke yourself (nor anyone else in the family). If that means giving up, suffer for the sake of your children and yourself. You'll feel virtuous, even if you feel wretched for a while.

- Start talking about it to your children when they are young, before teenage. They are more receptive, and it's just at the onset of puberty that most start experimenting with smoking.

- Encourage your children to develop fitness and strength. Think of this as a positive thing, rather than the negative of avoiding illness.

- Find role models amongst your teenager's friends who don't smoke. It will give your teenager someone of his or her own age to emulate.

- Don't spend too much time telling your teenager about the long-term harmful effects of smoking. They will have heard about it already, and threats of distant harm don't always mean much to teenagers. It can even be counter-productive.

- Don't make it easy for your teenager to smoke. Don't leave cigarettes around the house. Don't leave odd change around. Most teenagers will 'appropriate' loose money if they find it, and need it for something that you wouldn't approve of.

WHAT IF YOUR TEENAGER IS ALREADY SMOKING?

All of the above, and the following:

- Offer to help your teenager stop. It may take counselling. It may take blackmail and bribery. It will be painful, and he or she certainly needs your support and encouragement.

- Build on all the strengths your teenager may have. Encourage sport, or martial arts, or outdoor activities or hobbies. If your teenager is ready for it, suggest joining a gym, doing some weights training or working on body building. This could help your teenager feel proud of their body, and start to look after it.

- Many girls are worried that if they give up smoking, they will put on weight. They might, too, if they start eating instead of smoking. Help them to prevent this, perhaps with a review of foods eaten at home, or by involvement in an activities program. You might have to go for walks together, or find a dog that needs dog-walks. Or enrol her in an aerobics class.

- Help your teenager with developing social skills, if you feel that smoking had been a way of getting along with peers. You might help them develop strategies to open up conversations and respond to other teenagers. They might like to learn to dance. In some districts there are community groups for teenagers to develop social skills. Most people get along fine at parties without smoking, but for some it's difficult.

- Get your teenager to set a date to stop smoking — a date when you are available to be around, a date that friends know about and respect, a date when other stresses and strains (like exams) aren't going to interfere. Stick to that date: no postponements.

- Above all, if your teenager is a heavy smoker, recognize that nicotine is a powerful addiction, and it needs all the help possible to overcome it.

Alcohol: are they ready for it?

Steven and I were talking about all the harm he was doing to his body, what with late nights, skipped meals, and lack of exercise. He could fix all that, but what about drugs?

'I don't do drugs, Doc. Just alcohol.'

Steven didn't think he had an alcohol problem at all. He was 16, all his mates drank, his parents knew about it, he could handle it. He didn't even get bad hangovers. I suggested that his parents and I would probably agree that alcohol in moderation was not harmful to young adults and was socially enjoyable, but how many drinks would he have when he went out?

'Varies. About 12 stubbies. Maybe a bottle of whisky.'

'How often?'

'Friday and Saturday nights.'

'What about your liver and your brain cells and your judgment and the risk of doing something silly like picking a fight or having sex without a condom?'

Steven thought that was funny. 'Try telling that to a bunch of teenagers at a party.'

Teenage drinking, particularly binge drinking and getting drunk, is a major concern for parents and those interested in the health of young people. It is widespread and potentially destructive. For some it is addictive.

We live in a society in which alcohol is widely accepted, where social drinking is the norm, where alcohol is widely advertised. Most teenagers grow up in a family where one or both parents drink, at least on social occasions. Certainly there are many families who don't drink, for religious reasons, or because of personal conviction, or because they don't like it. Teenagers from such families, however, will probably have friends who drink regularly, and very few will have had no contact with drinking.

There is of course a major difference between families in which someone drinks to excess and risks their health and their family's happiness, and the majority of families who have alcohol in moderation and without harm to their health.

All of this will influence how teenagers behave towards alcohol. There is plenty of it around. It's easily available. It's an adult behaviour. It tastes good and makes you feel good.

How many teenagers drink?

There have been many surveys of young people in Australia. They tend to give a similar picture of teenage drinking. We have to consider those who drink moderately but regularly, and those who frequently become drunk through regular binge drinking.

Most people who drink started to do so while they were still at school. In Victoria, for example, about half of Year 11 students are drinking alcohol at least weekly. They start early in their teens. Fourteen per cent of Year 7 students, 36% of Year 9 students, and 50% of Year 11 students, are drinking regularly and on a weekly basis but are not heavy drinkers.

Binge drinking, in which students drink to excess (at least five drinks in a row at least fortnightly) is even commoner in older adolescents than in adults. In the same survey in Victorian schools, less than 1% of Year 7 students, 4% of Year 9 students, rising sharply to 18% of Year 11 students, were binge drinking. These figures are alarming.

Teenagers, when drunk, may lose some control of themselves and do risky things. Most teenagers when drunk are probably just happy and talkative. Some get easily

angered, and a few get violent. Quite a lot vomit, and a few manage to make themselves quite ill, especially if they combine alcohol with other drugs.

Teenagers are just starting on a career of drinking, and some will continue with this out-of-control drinking into their adult life. Most parents would prefer their teenager to drink, if they must, moderately and sensibly. Better still, of course, not at all. The trouble is that drinking is so common at teenage, as it is with adults, that it is probably just wishful thinking that we could stop them from drinking at least sometimes.

MANY PARENTS DON'T REALLY KNOW HOW MUCH THEIR TEENAGER IS DRINKING

Teenagers often protect a friend if they get drunk. They may ring up their friend's parents to ask if their friend can stay overnight after a party. They look after their friend for a few hours until he or she has stopped vomiting or has sobered up a bit. They might ring up their friend's older sibling to ask him or her to pick them up, rather than involve a parent.

WHAT CAN PARENTS DO IF THEIR TEENAGER DRINKS?

Parents should certainly make their views clear to their teenager. If they don't want their teenager to drink at all, they shouldn't make it easy for him or her to get alcohol, and they shouldn't allow it sometimes but not at others. This gives a confused message to the teenager.

Many people think that it is usually not realistic to try to stop teenagers drinking. This has led to the concept of 'harm minimization'. It means that rather than banning alcohol altogether, efforts should be made to make sure that it doesn't cause harm to the teenager. The harm it might cause includes emotional stress, the loss of self-respect and reputation, conflict with police or parents, vomiting and physical illness, and inappropriate sexual behaviour.

Strategies that parents might use are:

- Don't give your teenager any encouragement to drink.

- Try not to be judgmental about the drinking. If you make a moral issue about it, it might make your teenager defensive.

- Give your teenager the facts about alcohol and its possible harm. Then it becomes their responsibility to protect themselves.

- Give your teenager advice about practical issues, to keep them out of harm.

- Help your teenager work out what they feel is right for them.

- Help your teenager to know their limits.

- Give your teenager strategies to avoid sex when they have been drinking. A girl, for example, should stay with a group, not give any encouragement to a boy who is drunk and coming on too strongly. She may learn ways of saying 'No' with firmness and conviction.

- Work out how to get home safely after parties.

Marijuana

I got a phone call one evening about midnight. It was from a boy who had come to see me a few weeks before. At that time we had discussed his occasional use of marijuana, and whether it might have affected his asthma. Someone had told him it was good for asthma, because it relaxed the mind and the bronchial tubes. I had told him that was not the answer, because smoking anything has a bad effect on asthma, and there were much better and safer treatments anyway. We had discussed marijuana, and I had said that it wasn't as harmless as he thought. We talked about some of the possible bad effects.

The phone call was distressing. 'You were right about the dope. I've blown my mind, Doc. My body's weird, I'm scared. Nothing's like it should be. I think I'm going mad. What's going to happen to me?'

We settled how he was going to get home safely with the help of a friend. I told him that the effects would wear off soon. But: no more alcohol, no more of any other drugs, and certainly no more marijuana tonight (I actually hoped that would apply to every other night in future, but this wasn't the time for lectures. He was very frightened.) We arranged that he would come to see me next day.

Not all parents realize this, but adolescents live in a teenage society in which marijuana is part of the everyday scene, is often easily obtainable, is widely accepted and liked. A survey of Australian teenagers showed that 44% of them, by the time they have left school, have tried marijuana, and 13% of Year 11 students are using it regularly. A youth told me recently that it was actually easier to get than alcohol.

'Anyone can get you marijuana. A lot of school-aged kids deal in it: it's a way of supporting their habit. Twenty dollars will buy you and one or two of your friends an evening of dope. You go to a party, and someone will offer it, either to try or to buy. You can often get it free.'

This is very different from the party scene that many parents of teenagers remember. A survey reported in Victoria showed that the proportion of adults who had tried marijuana fell with age, and in the 45-year-old and over group, only 8% had ever used it. It means that the views that parents and teenagers hold about marijuana may be very different. It also means that the laws about marijuana, and family and school rules, are broken so often that they may not be taken seriously by teenagers, except the slight possibility of being found out and punished.

I was asked to talk about some aspects of health to about two hundred Year 12 students recently. Someone asked me my views on whether marijuana should be legalized. They had recently had a talk from someone who had suggested that legalization would have many benefits: it would 'decriminalize' something that many of the group had done or would do; it would show people who feared marijuana that it was no worse than alcohol or tobacco, and probably less harmful to society as a whole. It has been decriminalized in some states already.

I asked the group to give their own opinion by voting on the issue. There was some hesitancy, but the big majority voted in favour of legalizing it.

WHAT'S GOOD ABOUT MARIJUANA?

For most people, smoking marijuana gives a feeling of wellbeing, of pleasure and happiness. It makes them relaxed and more sociable and talkative. It doesn't do this for everyone, nor does it have the same effect every time it's used. Much depends on the company and the surroundings and how a person feels at the time.

There are lots of arguments in favour of marijuana and its legalization. After all, it's hard to enforce a law that almost half the student population have broken at some time during their school days, and many will continue to break. It's not a particularly anti-social drug like alcohol, which may make people reckless and violent, or heroin, which is a major cause of crime in our society. It doesn't seem to cause nearly as much physical harm to the user as tobacco. It isn't addictive in the same way as heroin or alcohol or tobacco. Since most adolescents seem to want something that enhances personal relationships and makes them feel happy and relaxed, you could argue that marijuana is the least harmful of all the available drugs.

WHAT ARE SOME OF THE BAD THINGS ABOUT MARIJUANA?

What are the harmful effects? The acute effects include a dry mouth, bloodshot eyes, increased heart rate and raised blood pressure. (Teenagers disguise the bloodshot eyes by putting in eye drops or wearing dark glasses.) The main concerns, however, are the mental effects, which are a particular danger for those who use marijuana regularly. These effects include mental impairment with reduced short-term memory (very destructive to school learning).

Teenagers who are stoned may be less coordinated (sport coaches aren't in favour of it), and may lose their sense of time. Driving can become a danger, much as alcohol affects judgment and a quick coordinated response to a road crisis.

Heavy doses may lead to psychotic attacks, including schizophrenia. Eventually people may become dependent on the drug for their happiness: they may need it to get through their day at school or to cope with life or to enjoy parties.

There is some evidence that long-term use may lead to impairment of the immune system which helps ward off disease. If this is so, it is similar to several other drugs that have been blamed for increasing the risks of contracting serious illness.

Probably the most worrying thing for regular users is that they may lose their motivation to do anything. School work doesn't matter, study can be put off, lessons become a hazy blur, and if they are sent out of school they don't care. Very few chronic users actually succeed in the challenging professions. But you might say that most people don't want to, so it's part of making personal decisions. The tragedy could be that a bright young teenager doesn't achieve his or her full potential at a critical time of life, when a choice of career may depend so much on success at school, and the chance of getting into a good university course may be lost forever.

Some teenagers go to school stoned most days. Either they smoke dope on the way to school or they are still affected from smoking the night before. It may help get them through the day, but it sure doesn't help with school performance. Most intelligent teenagers know perfectly well that marijuana affects judgment, learning and motivation, and that it hangs around long after the high has worn off.

In discussing this with the group of Year 12 students, who were a thoughtful and intelligent group, it was suggested that legalizing marijuana might give the message to younger teenagers that it was O.K. to use. Even if the law stated that it was only legal after the age, say, of 18, it would still suggest that society accepted it. Opium was legal in many Western countries until people realized that it was potentially dangerous and very addictive, which led to its being declared illegal.

We didn't take another vote, but there were some who came up afterwards and said that from their experience, they agreed it wasn't a harmless drug.

WHAT CAN PARENTS DO IF THEY THINK THEIR TEENAGER IS SMOKING MARIJUANA?

Talk about it. Give your views. Avoid a purely moral standpoint, because that may not be very persuasive to a teenager whose friends all smoke it. The legal aspect may carry some weight, but the fact is that teenagers don't seem to suffer much from the law if they just smoke marijuana at private parties. It's very different in public places, including school and discos and public functions.

If you, as parents, don't approve of marijuana and don't use it yourselves, don't allow it in your house — particularly if your teenager is having friends over or is having a party. Make this clear, enforce it, and send home any of your teenager's friends who are caught smoking marijuana.

If, despite this, you think that your teenager is using marijuana regularly and it is having a bad effect, take them for professional advice. Get in before it does much harm.

CHAPTER 11

LAST WORD

On leaving home . . . and coming back

Just when they seem to have become livable with, and are starting to be responsible and have a job, they announce that they are going to leave home.

All the hassles of adolescence are forgotten. They appreciate your help in getting started in their new lives, they take some of your saucepans and plates and send you off to buy them a broom. They find a place to live in, and say they'll come and see you when they have settled down.

Is this the end? Has your marathon task of rearing a human being come to a close? Can you settle back to do all the things you would like (assuming that you haven't got a few more little monsters at home waiting to give you an interesting journey through their teenage years)?

No. They reappear. They come back. They return with their washing. They come at meal times. They check what's in the fridge, and probably eat it. They want to wash their car at your place because there isn't a hose at theirs. They bring their cat over for you to look after while they go on holidays. They expect you to preserve their rooms intact: after all, it *is* their room, and it still has all their stuff in it. They need to check you out. They want to know if you are alright. Don't tell them that you have been a bit run down, or have had a few headaches, or they will make you see a doctor. They may even threaten to come with you to make sure that you do what you're told.

If you're not careful, they will force a role reversal on you, and start telling you what to do, just like you did with them only a few years before. And of course, if there are any little brothers or sisters still at home, they will tell you how to avoid making the same mistakes again that you did with them.

And if that isn't enough, they move back home from time to time. 'Just for a while, until I find a new place.'

Being a parent doesn't end when your children stop being teenagers and grow up. But it does get more peaceful. And it was all worthwhile.

REFERENCES

Centre for Adolescent Health Melbourne Publication, *Adolescent Health Survey 1992*, March 1993.

Dietz, W. H. and Gortmaker, S. L., 'Do we fatten our children at the television set? Obesity and television viewing in children and adolescents', *Paediatrics*, 1995, vol. 75, pp. 807–812.

Health and Community Services, *Health Status of Victorian Children and Young People*, 1994.

Health and Community Services, *School Students and Drug Use*, 1993.

Health and Community Services, *Victorian Drug Strategy Unit*, 1993.

Hill, D., White, V., Williams, R., Gardner, G., 'Tobacco and Alcohol use among Australian Secondary School Students in 1990', *Medical J Australia*, 1993, vol. 158, pp. 225–233.

Rolls, B. J., 'Food beliefs and food choices in adolescents', *Medical J Australia*, 1988, vol. 148, pp. S9–S13.

Truswell, A. S., Dainton-Hill, I., 'Food habits of adolescents', *Nutrition Reviews*, 1981, vol. 39, pp. 73–88.

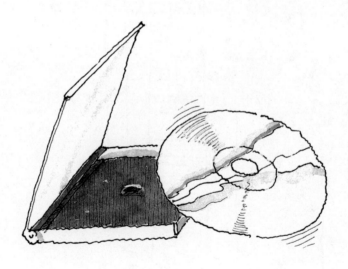

INDEX